Victory
Secrets

Dag Heward-Mills

Parchment House

VICTORY SECRETS

First published 2017 by Parchment House
2nd Printing 2018

Find out more about Dag Heward-Mills at:

ᵀHealing Jesus Campaign
Email: evangelist@daghewardmills.org
Website: www.daghewardmills.org
Facebook: Dag Heward-Mills
Twitter: @EvangelistDag

ISBN : 978-1-68398-196-1

Contents

VICTORY SECRET NO.1

What is a Victory Secret?

Hast thou heard THE SECRET OF GOD? And dost thou restrain wisdom to thyself?

Job 15:8

A victory secret is a secret that will make you into a living wonder! A victory secret is the secret of God!

Have you heard the secret of God? Have you read the secret of God? Have you been exposed to the secret of God? The hidden wisdom of God is the secret of God! Have you received the wisdom of God? Have you received revelation from above? If you have not heard the secret of God, you have missed what you really need. The secret of God is the wisdom of God in a mystery that is ordained for your glory and beautification.

But we speak the wisdom of God in a mystery, even the hidden wisdom, which God ordained before the world unto our glory:

1 Corinthians 2:7

What you need is not earthly wisdom. Earthly wisdom is the teaching of economics, law, maths, science, accounting etc. All these secular subjects are nice but they are earthly human wisdom. There is a place for all those things. But it has no place in the church. In the church, we have something far higher "And my speech and my preaching was not with enticing words of *man's wisdom...*" (1 Corinthians 2:4). There is a far greater kind of wisdom that comes from God. The wisdom of God contains the secret of God. That is what you need for your life. "But we speak the wisdom of God in a mystery, even the hidden wisdom, which God ordained before the world unto our glory" (1 Corinthians 2:7). This kind of wisdom has been ordained to make you glorious and to turn you into a living wonder.

Let us look at the wonderful benefits of discovering the secret of God.

Six Reasons Why You Must Discover the Secret of God

1. Life and death depend on your discovery of the secret of God:

The king answered and said, I know of certainty that ye would gain the time, because ye see the thing is gone from me. But if ye will not make known unto me the dream, there is but one decree for you: for ye have prepared lying and corrupt words to speak before me, till the time be changed: therefore tell me the dream, and I shall know that ye can shew me the interpretation thereof.

The Chaldeans answered before the king, and said, There is not a man upon the earth that can shew the king's matter: therefore there is no king, lord, nor ruler, that asked such things at any magician, or astrologer, or Chaldean. And it is a rare thing that the king requireth, and there is none other that can shew it before the king, except the gods, whose dwelling is not with flesh. For this cause the king was angry and very furious, and commanded to destroy all the wise men of Babylon. And the decree went forth that THE WISE MEN SHOULD BE SLAIN; and THEY SOUGHT DANIEL AND HIS FELLOWS TO BE SLAIN.

Then Daniel went in, and desired of the king that he would give him time, and that he would shew the king the interpretation. Then Daniel went to his house, and made the thing known to Hananiah, Mishael, and Azariah, his companions: THAT THEY WOULD DESIRE MERCIES OF THE GOD OF HEAVEN CONCERNING THIS SECRET; THAT DANIEL AND HIS FELLOWS SHOULD NOT PERISH WITH THE REST OF THE

WISE MEN OF BABYLON. THEN WAS THE SECRET REVEALED UNTO DANIEL in a night vision. Then Daniel blessed the God of heaven. Daniel answered and said, Blessed be the name of God for ever and ever: for wisdom and might are his: And he changeth the times and the seasons: he removeth kings, and setteth up kings: he giveth wisdom unto the wise, and knowledge to them that know understanding: HE REVEALETH THE DEEP AND SECRET THINGS: he knoweth what is in the darkness, and the light dwelleth with him.

Daniel 2:8-13, 16-22

Daniel and his companions were in great danger of being executed. Death was staring at them in the face. The king knew that most of the wise men, astrologers and magicians were hypocrites, full of deception. King Nebuchadnezzar desperately wanted to clear his palace of all imposters. The test that the king instituted would ensure that only genuinely wise people would remain in his palace as advisers. To be a good adviser, you need to know certain secrets. There are secrets behind every great achievement and behind every great person.

Often, we wrongly speculate about what has made a person great. Most of the time we do not really know the secret of someone's greatness. Discovering certain secrets will prevent you from perishing. The spirit of knowledge is also the Spirit of God. "...When the enemy shall come in like a flood, the Spirit of the Lord shall lift up a standard against him" (Isaiah 59:19). When the enemy comes in to kill you, the spirit of knowledge lifts up a standard against him. The word 'standard' is the Hebrew word "nus" which means "to cause to disappear". Through knowledge, certain things are caused to disappear. Years ago, everyone who developed malaria, asthma, high blood pressure or diabetes simply died of these diseases. Through knowledge, these diseases have been "caused to disappear" and been neutralized.

Life and death may depend on your knowledge of certain secrets. There are secrets that are very important for your life. Anyone who has been blessed to enjoy the secrets of God knows that life and death virtually depend on their knowledge of certain secrets. This is why you need to seek revelation from God. Your knowledge of a secret will make you have the upper hand. All the advances of science, medicine, astronomy, agriculture, mechanics and physics are based on secrets that have been discovered. Those secrets are facts that have existed for thousands of years. Inventors are basically discoverers of secrets. E has always been equal to mc^2. Einstein was only the discoverer of a secret that had existed for thousands of years.

A victory secret is a revelation that brings you the victory! Victory secrets are revelations from the Holy Spirit that can make the difference in your life's work and ministry. Often, the difference between life and death is a little knowledge. God can grant you knowledge today! God can cause you to know a little secret that will change everything about your life and ministry. Some people call these key snippets of knowledge a "revelation". Whatever you call it, these victory secrets will lead to great victories and triumphs.

Many good examples of the effects of victory secrets can be found in history books. In the fourteenth century, a disease called "the Plague" entered the world and consumed millions of people. Many people died and entire populations were wiped out. The fear of this illness persisted for years as the Plague continued to resurface in different parts of the world, terrorizing the population and wiping out large groups of people.

Indeed, early Modern Europe experienced the worst human disaster in European history, when the Plague hit Europe in 1347. This bubonic plague actually wiped out a third of the population of Europe. Can you imagine a disease that spreads throughout a continent and wipes out a third of its population? Even in modern times, when the Ebola virus spread through Sierra Leone, Liberia and Guinea, only ten thousand people died. Imagine a disease that could wipe out millions of people and "empty" a continent of its population.

Plague victims had a very low chance of surviving due to symptoms such as high fevers, and internal bleeding, which would cause black spots and large tumours. Anyone who contracted the disease died within three to five days.

The doctors of the day thought the plague was created by air corrupted by humid weather, decaying unburied bodies and poor sanitation. Some people also thought the disease was being spread by Jews. The medical doctors of the fourteenth century did not know that the disease came through a simple bacteria carried by fleas and rats. The medical profession did not know about simple antibiotics! They had absolutely no way of fighting the disease. Knowledge of the secret of antibiotics would have delivered millions of people from death.

[1]It was not until 1877 that Louis Pasteur and Robert Koch observed that an airborne *bacillus* could inhibit the growth of another bacteria, *bacillus anthracis*. This phenomenon exhibited by anti-bacterial drugs was called *antibiosis*. It was only in 1942 when drugs that acted that way were eventually named *antibiotics* by an American microbiologist, Seiman Waksman.[1]

It was this secret of antibiotics that was absent in the fourteenth century! This is the secret that would have prevented millions of people from perishing at the hands of the bubonic plague in the fourteenth century. Simple drugs like *streptomycin, gentamicin* and *ciprofloxacin* would have stopped the disease in its tracks. Today, your chances of dying from the bubonic plague are almost zero.

Not even one person would have died from the bubonic plague if we had had the secret of antibiotics. A victory secret greatly transforms lives. A victory secret saves many lives. A victory secret changes everything.

One of the most important prayers of your life must be the prayer for the spirit of revelation. Pray for victory secrets! That is the prayer for timely revelation and knowledge that will make the difference in your life.

2. **Your prosperity depends on your discovery of the secret of God:**

Thus saith the Lord to his anointed, to Cyrus, whose right hand I have holden, to subdue nations before him; and I will loose the loins of kings, to open before him the two leaved gates; and the gates shall not be shut;

I will go before thee, and make the crooked places straight: I will break in pieces the gates of brass, and cut in sunder the bars of iron:

And I will give thee the TREASURES OF DARKNESS, and HIDDEN RICHES OF SECRET PLACES, that thou mayest know that I, the Lord, which call thee by thy name, am the God of Israel.

Isaiah 45:1-3

Victory secrets will lead you to prosperity. Most riches are hidden from view. Most real riches are hidden away from view. That is why they are called "treasures of darkness". Most of the riches in our world are hidden in secret places. To find the riches of this world, you will need to be given revelation to unlock the secret of how to locate wealth. You will need to discover the secret places where wealth is hidden.

Why some people are rich still remains a mystery to many. People do many things in order to prosper, but few are given the secret of prosperity. Money is locked up in secret places. Without the knowledge of certain secrets, you will live in poverty for the rest of your life. You need the spirit of revelation to give you the secrets of prosperity and of success. Church growth is released through your knowledge of certain secrets. All of our difficulties can be brought to an abrupt end if we discover the secret behind true success.

You need to discover secrets because greatness and prosperity are based on the discovery of important secrets. People who have invented cars, aeroplanes, electronic tablets (such as the iPad), phones and televisions are the millionaires of our world. Many nations do not know the secrets of how to make these things work. Those who have discovered these secrets have become the richest people in the world. Consider the vast difference that exists between those who have discovered the secret of making a mobile phone and those who simply harvest tomatoes and oranges. You do not need any special secret to harvest coconuts or pepper. But you do need to know certain secrets to make a television work. Knowing secrets makes people very valuable. Not only was Daniel kept alive, but he also became the third most important person in town and received prosperity symbolized by a gold chain that was put around his neck. When you discover the secret of God through the spirit of revelation, you will also become important. You will be covered with gold, by the spirit of revelation.

> **Then commanded Belshazzar, and they clothed Daniel with scarlet, and put a chain of gold about his neck, and made a proclamation concerning him, that he should be the third ruler in the kingdom.**
>
> **Daniel 5:29**

3. **The secret of God is given to the righteous and to His prophets.**

> **For the froward is abomination to the Lord: but his secret is with the righteous.**
>
> **Proverbs 3:32**

You do not tell your secrets to everyone. Why do you expect God to tell His secrets to everyone? The people to whom God has given His secret are those He sees as righteous. God withholds His revelation from people who are wicked and gives them to the righteous.

Servants are close to their masters and work around their space. It is therefore not strange that servants know many secrets that outsiders will never know. Strive to be a servant of God and strive to be His prophet and you are guaranteed a rich supply of wonderful secrets.

Surely the Lord God will do nothing, but he revealeth his secret unto his servants the prophets.

Amos 3:7

4. **The secret of God is given at special seasons of your life:**

Oh that I were as in months past, as in the days when God preserved me;

When his candle shined upon my head, and when by his light I walked through darkness;

As I was IN THE DAYS OF MY YOUTH, WHEN THE SECRET OF GOD was upon my tabernacle;

Job 29:2-4

Job enjoyed knowing some of these secrets at a certain season of his life. He spoke passionately about the season when God gave him secrets and revelation. You will always look back to the season when God gave you certain revelations.

Job desperately wanted to experience the times of revelation again. True prophets will tell you when they have a revelation and when they do not. The reality is that revelation does not come all the time. Job was saying he wished he were young again, when the secrets of God were being revealed to him (Job 29:4).

Kenneth Hagin described how God blessed him with eight visions of Jesus Christ between 1950 and 1958. He described how the Lord did not appear to him in that way any more from 1958 onwards. Kenneth Hagin was only thirty-three years old when the Lord appeared to him. He ministered until he was eighty-six years old.

It is important to discover secrets as a young person. When you are young, your whole life is ahead of you. You have a good chance of implementing the secrets and revelations that God shows you. I discovered the secret of Matthew 6:33 when I was in school. It has been the greatest secret of prosperity for my life. Seeking God first and building His kingdom first are divine secrets to prosperity!

5. Prayer is the key to discovering important secrets of God:

Then Daniel went to his house, and made the thing known to Hananiah, Mishael, and Azariah, his companions: THAT THEY WOULD DESIRE MERCIES OF THE GOD OF HEAVEN CONCERNING THIS SECRET; that Daniel and his fellows should not perish with the rest of the wise men of Babylon.
THEN WAS THE SECRET REVEALED UNTO DANIEL IN A NIGHT VISION. Then Daniel blessed the God of heaven. Daniel answered and said, Blessed be the name of God for ever and ever: for wisdom and might are his: And he changeth the times and the seasons: he removeth kings, and setteth up kings: he giveth wisdom unto the wise, and knowledge to them that know understanding: He revealeth the deep and secret things: he knoweth what is in the darkness, and the light dwelleth with him. I thank thee, and praise thee, O thou God of my fathers, who hast given me wisdom and might, and hast made known unto me now what we desired of thee: for thou hast now made known unto us the king's matter.

Daniel 2:17-23

When Daniel and his team needed to know certain secrets, they prayed about it. He asked God to show them mercy. God gave them the secret to what they needed to know. Apostle Paul prayed for the spirit of revelation. He prayed, that the God of our Lord Jesus Christ, the Father of glory, might give a spirit of wisdom and of revelation in the knowledge of Him (Ephesians 1:17). Prayer is the master key to discovering important secrets of your life.

6. **Meditation is the master key to the discovery of the secret of God:**

    O how love I thy law! It is my meditation all the day. Thou through thy commandments hast made me wiser than mine enemies: for they are ever with me. I have more understanding than all my teachers: for thy testimonies are my meditation. I understand more than the ancients, because I keep thy precepts.

    Thy word is a lamp unto my feet, and a light unto my path.

    Psalm 119:97-100, 105

    The Word of God is a lamp and a light. When light comes on, all secrets are revealed. Whatever is lying in darkness is exposed and brought out into full view. Loving the Law of God and meditating on it day and night is your master key to the discovery of the secrets you need.

The Secret of the Spirit of Revelation

Wherefore I also, after I heard of your faith in the Lord Jesus, and love unto all the saints, cease not to give thanks for you, making mention of you in my prayers;

That the God of our Lord Jesus Christ, the Father of glory, may give unto you THE SPIRIT OF WISDOM AND REVELATION in the knowledge of him: the eyes of your understanding being enlightened; that ye may know what is the hope of his calling, and what the riches of the glory of his inheritance in the saints.

Ephesians 1:15-18

The book of Revelation clearly reveals and unveils things that are hidden from open view. Things that are not public knowledge are made known to us if we care to accept them. Revelation means to unveil and to show something that is hidden.

What is the Spirit of Revelation?

The spirit of revelation leads to the unfolding, the opening and the uncovering of what is going on behind the scenes. The spirit of revelation shows you what is going on behind the curtains. The spirit of revelation teaches you all about what is under the covers. The spirit of revelation gives knowledge that is a pre-requisite for many great accomplishments. The spirit of revelation always marks the beginning of great ministries.

The spirit of revelation often manifests as visions and dreams. These visions and dreams show you what is happening behind the scenes. The spirit of revelation can also lead you to have experiences that make you see things, hear things and know things that few people ever experience, see or hear. When you are honoured to see, hear and know secrets, you are experiencing the spirit of revelation. The apostle, John, had these two different manifestations of the spirit of revelation.

Most people do not recognize when God is giving them the spirit of revelation because they only want His revelation to come through fantastic visions. It is true that John was taken to the island of Patmos and there he was transported to heaven to have fantastic visions and dreams. On the other hand, he had the amazing experience of being close to Jesus to see, to look upon and to touch Jesus Christ. This physical experience gave him a great revelation of who Jesus Christ was and launched him into his ministry. Apostle John's ministry was launched through the revelation of Jesus Christ. Apostle John's latter ministry was established by his visions of heaven and eternity.

The Spirit of Revelation is the Door to Ministry

1. **The first revelation of Apostle John:** The spirit of revelation was the basis of Apostle John's ministry.

    That which was from the beginning, which WE HAVE HEARD, which WE HAVE SEEN with our eyes, which WE HAVE LOOKED UPON, and OUR HANDS have handled, of the Word of life;

    That which we have seen and heard declare we unto you, that ye also may have fellowship with us: and truly our fellowship is with the Father, and with his Son Jesus Christ.

    1 John 1:1, 3

    This revelation marked the birth of John's ministry. This revelation was not a vision. It was what I call a *"real life revelation"*. What John had seen, experienced and touched was just as important as the vision he was to have later in his life and ministry.

    The people I have met, the things I have seen, the encounters I have had are all part of the revelation God has given me. Each encounter is a vision that makes me see more and understand more. On several occasions, I have sat with men of God who spoke freely about their lives and ministries. There were times I would wonder, "Why is this man telling me all these things? How did I come to be in this privileged place to see, to hear and to know things which are kept secret from the general public?"

    That was when I realised that I had been given the spirit of revelation, just like John, to see things with my eyes, to look upon certain things, to hear certain things.

    I once had lunch with a great man of God whom I had only heard of from the newspapers. He shared the secrets of his marriage and explained how he ended up divorced. I was amazed at the things I heard. I learnt a lot and I realised I was being given a spirit of revelation.

On another occasion, I spent two hours with a famous American preacher who told me amazing things that had gone on in his life and the American ministry. He described terrible mistakes he had made and said, "On hindsight we should have done certain things…"

I was amazed at the "certain things" he said he should have done in the ministry. I knew he would never publicly advise people to do those "certain things". It was advice I was privileged to hear from a very experienced and very famous person. Indeed, this was the spirit of revelation at work, telling me and showing me the secret things that are covered in great ministries.

Only few are ever privileged to see and hear certain things. Apostle John described his experience with the spirit of revelation. He said he had seen certain things, he had heard certain things, he had looked upon certain things, and his hands had handled certain things. What he had seen, heard and touched was exactly what he was sharing. Most new ministries are born out of the spirit of revelation!

The famous books of John - first, second and third John are the fruits of the spirit of revelation that John had through *"real life revelations"*.

2.   **The second revelation of Apostle John:** The spirit of revelation was the basis of Apostle John's ministry.

The Revelation of Jesus Christ, which God gave unto him, to shew unto his servants things which must shortly come to pass; and he sent and signified it by his angel unto his servant John:

Revelation 1:1

John was also given amazing revelation through visions. The famous book of Revelation is the fruit of the spirit of revelation that John had through his visions and dreams. This revelation gave rise to his book-writing ministry which has lasted for two thousand years. Today, it is the revelation of John that is perhaps most relevant to the current events of our world. The revelation that John had is playing out before our very eyes.

3. **The revelation of Peter:** The spirit of revelation was the basis of Peter's ministry.

    He saith unto them, But whom say ye that I am? And Simon Peter answered and said, Thou art the Christ, the Son of the living God. And Jesus answered and said unto him, Blessed art thou, Simon Barjona: for FLESH AND BLOOD HATH NOT REVEALED IT UNTO THEE, BUT MY FATHER WHICH IS IN HEAVEN.

    And I say also unto thee, that thou art Peter, and upon this rock I will build my church; and the gates of hell shall not prevail against it.

    Matthew 16:15-18

    God revealed to Peter who Jesus was. Jesus probed and searched to find out if Peter had received the spirit of revelation. You can find out if someone has the spirit of revelation by listening to the person speak. Peter's revelation of who Jesus was, marked the beginning of his worldwide ministry as the head of the Church. Once he had received the revelation that Jesus was the Son of God, he qualified to have his worldwide ministry. His revelation was the reason for his appointment. Your revelation will be reason for your appointment. That is why you must be willing to search the scriptures, to study the Word, to meditate until God gives you the spirit of revelation.

4. **The revelation of Paul:** The spirit of revelation was the basis of Paul's ministry.

    And lest I should be exalted above measure through the ABUNDANCE OF THE REVELATIONS, there was given to me a thorn in the flesh, the messenger of Satan to buffet me, lest I should be exalted above measure.

    2 Corinthians 12:7

Paul had the spirit of revelation as well. He described himself as having an abundance of revelations. It is this abundance of revelations that Paul experienced that launched him into the ministry. The abundance of his revelations led to the great ministry that he had. Paul appreciated the spirit of revelation and the effects of this spirit. That is why he prayed earnestly for people to receive the spirit of revelation in the knowledge of Christ.

5.   **The revelation of Samuel:** The spirit of revelation was the basis of Samuel's ministry.

Now Samuel did not yet know the Lord, NEITHER WAS THE WORD OF THE LORD YET REVEALED UNTO HIM.

1 Samuel 3:7

The famous prophet Samuel was not able to begin his ministry because he had not yet received a revelation. Notice how the scripture puts it – "the word of the Lord was not yet revealed unto him"! When the word of the Lord is revealed to you, your ministry will start. Knowing God for yourself and having a personal revelation from the Lord is the signal for the beginning of your ministry. When you have not been given your own personal revelation, you are expected to grow up on the revelation given to others.

Most of us have not been given the revelation that was given to Apostle Paul. We are therefore expected to be nurtured and grow in the Lord as we study the revelation given to him. It is interesting to see pastors starting their own ministries because they want to be called "founders" and "presidents". Many of these people are like Samuel to whom the word of the Lord has not been revealed. They do not have the revelation that initiates a ministry. To run ahead and start things when no revelation has been given to you is a mistake. Until a revelation has been given to you, you must stand on, and grow on the revelation that has been given to others. "But I certify you, brethren, that the gospel which was preached of me is not after man. For I neither received it of man, neither was I taught it, but by the revelation of Jesus Christ" (Galatians 1:11-12). Revelations are from God and they are a mark of the Holy Spirit on any one who receives it.

6.   The revelation of Daniel: The spirit of revelation was the basis of Daniel's ministry.

The excellent spirit that was found in Daniel is the spirit of revelation. Daniel had so much of the spirit of revelation; and this is why he functioned as a prophet under king Nebuchadnezzar and also under his son king Belshazzar.

On the day Daniel was appointed to king Belshazzar's team of advisers, great reference was made to the spirit of revelation working in Daniel's ministry. He knew secrets and understood things that were kept hidden from others.

There is a man in thy kingdom, in whom is the spirit of the holy gods; and in the days of thy father LIGHT AND UNDERSTANDING AND WISDOM, like the wisdom of the gods, was found in him; whom the king Nebuchadnezzar thy father, the king, I say, thy father, made master of the magicians, astrologers, Chaldeans, and soothsayers; FORASMUCH AS AN EXCELLENT SPIRIT, AND KNOWLEDGE, AND UNDERSTANDING, INTERPRETING OF DREAMS, AND SHEWING OF HARD SENTENCES, AND DISSOLVING OF DOUBTS, were found in the same Daniel, whom the king named Belteshazzar: now let Daniel be called, and he will shew the interpretation.

Daniel 5:11-12

Revelations will always be the basis of ministry. Daniel had visions and dreams about many things. Daniel had visions and dreams about four winged beasts that came out of the sea. Daniel also had a vision about a ram with two horns. Daniel's ability to see, to know and to understand was the working of this spirit.

7.   **The revelation of Joseph:** The spirit of revelation was the basis of Joseph's ministry.

> Then spake the chief butler unto Pharaoh, saying, I do remember my faults this day: Pharaoh was wroth with his servants, and put me in ward in the captain of the guard's house, both me and the chief baker: And we dreamed a dream in one night, I and he; we dreamed each man according to the interpretation of his dream. And there was there with us a young man, an Hebrew, servant to the captain of the guard; and we told him, and HE INTERPRETED TO US OUR DREAMS; to each man according to his dream he did interpret.
>
> Genesis 41:9-12

Joseph was called out of the prison because of the spirit of revelation. Someone remembered that he had the spirit of revelation and was able to understand difficult things and explain things that were hidden from others. *Joseph was launched into his world ministry through the spirit of revelation at work in his life.* Pray for the spirit of revelation! Through that spirit, you will be launched into the most important aspects of your life and ministry. Study the Word of God, pray for the spirit of revelation and God will show you what to do.

It is when a person has great revelation that he is launched into ministry. It is the revelations that he has that are the basis of his ministry. Religion has been defined as a response to a revelation. This is why people without a certain level of revelation should not start movements. When you are not given a certain revelation you are often not qualified to be a founder or a pioneer.

8.   **The revelation of Kenneth Hagin:**   The spirit of revelation was the basis of Kenneth Hagin's ministry.

Kenneth E. Hagin was launched into his worldwide ministry by the revelation that he had of Jesus Christ. The eight visions that he had of Jesus Christ between 1950 and 1958 formed the basis of his prophetic ministry. The revelations that I have received about certain things form the basis of my ministry today.

9.   **The revelation of William Booth:** The spirit of revelation was the basis of William Booth's ministry.

Churches and movements must write and protect the revelations through which they were birthed. Many great churches were founded on revelation because ministries are birthed through revelation. Today however, the revelations that gave birth to some great ministries are no longer even associated with those ministries. The great servant of God, William Booth, had amazing visions that revealed to him the importance of the salvation of souls. This revelation was the basis on which he launched his Salvation Army. William Booth shared a great vision that birthed his mission.

Let us enjoy this amazing vision by William Booth.

The Vision that Birthed William Booth's Ministry

[2]*"I saw a dark and stormy ocean. Over it the black clouds hung heavily; through them every now and then vivid lightnings flashed and loud thunders rolled, while the winds moaned and the waves rose and foamed and fretted and broke and rose to foam and fret and break again.*

In that ocean I thought I saw myriads of poor human beings plunging and floating and shouting and shrieking and cursing and struggling and drowning; and as they cursed and shrieked, they rose and shrieked again and then sank to rise no more.

And out of this dark, angry ocean I saw a mighty rock that rose up with its summit towering high above the black clouds that overhung the stormy sea; and all round the base of this rock I saw a vast platform; and onto this platform I saw with delight a number of the poor, struggling, drowning wretches continually climbing out of the angry ocean; and I saw that a number of those who were already safe on the platform were helping the poor creatures still in the angry waters to reach the same place of safety.

On looking more closely, I found a number of those who had been rescued scheming and contriving by ladders and ropes and boats and other expedients more effectually to deliver the poor strugglers out of this sea. Here and there were some who actually jumped into the water regardless of all consequences, in their eagerness to "rescue the perishing"; and I hardly know which gladdened me most – the sight of the poor people climbing on to the rocks and so reaching the place of safety or the devotion and self-sacrifice of those whose whole being was wrapped up in efforts for their deliverance.

And as I looked, I saw that the occupants of that platform were quite a mixed company. That is, they were divided into different "sets" or castes and occupied themselves with different pleasures and employments; but only a very few of them seemed to make it their business to get the people out of the sea.

But what puzzled me most was the fact that though all had been rescued at one time or another from the ocean, nearly everyone seemed to have forgotten all about it. Anyway, the memory of its darkness and danger no longer troubled them. Then what was equally strange and perplexing to me was that these people did not seem to have any care – that is, any agonizing care – about the poor perishing ones who were struggling and drowning before their eyes, many of who were their own husbands and wives and mothers and sisters and children.

And this unconcern could not have been the result of ignorance, because they lived right in sight of it all and talked about it sometimes and regularly went to hear lectures in which the awful state of the poor drowning creatures was described.

I have already said that the occupants of this platform were engaged in different pursuits. Some of them were absorbed night and day in trading, in order to make gain, storing up their savings in boxes, strong rooms, and the like.

Many spent their time in amusing themselves with growing flowers on the side of the rock; others in painting pieces of cloth, or in playing music, or in dressing themselves up in different styles and walking about to be admired.

Some occupied themselves chiefly in eating and drinking. Others were greatly taken up with arguing about the poor drowning creatures in the sea, and as to what would become of them in the future while many contented themselves that they did their duty to the perishing creatures by the performance of curious religious ceremonies.

On looking more closely, I found that some of the crowd who had reached the place of safety had discovered a passage up the rock leading to a higher platform still, which was fairly above the black clouds that overhung the ocean, and from which they had a good view of the mainland not very far away, and to which they expected to be taken off at some distant day. Here they passed their time in pleasant thoughts, congratulating themselves and one another on their good fortune in being rescued from the stormy deep and singing songs about the happiness that would be theirs when they should be taken to the mainland, which they imagined they could plainly distinguish just "over there".

And all this time the struggling, shrieking multitudes were floating about in the dark sea, quite nearby – so near that they could easily have been rescued. Instead they were perishing in full view, not only one by one but sinking down in shoals, every day, in the angry water.

And as I looked, I found that the handful of people on the platform I had observed before were still struggling with their rescue work – oh, God! How I wished there had been a multitude of them! Indeed, these toilers seemed to do little else but fret and weep and toil and scheme for the perishing people. They gave themselves no rest and sadly bothered everyone they could get at around them by persistently entreating them to come to their assistance. In fact, they came to be voted a real nuisance by many quite benevolent and kind-hearted people and by some who were very religious too. But still they went on, spending all they had, and all they could get, on boats and rafts and drags and ropes and every other imaginable device they could invent for saving the poor, wretched, drowning people.

And then I saw something more wonderful still. The miseries and agonies and perils and blasphemies of these poor struggling people in this dark sea moved the pity of the great God in heaven so much that He sent a Great Being to deliver them. And I thought that this Great Being whom Jehovah sent came straight from His palace, right through the black clouds, and leaped right into the raging sea among the drowning, sinking people; and there I saw Him toiling to rescue them, with tears and cries, until the sweat of His great anguish ran down in blood. And as He *toiled and embraced the poor wretches and tried to lift them on to the rock, He was continually crying to those already rescued – to those He had helped up with His own bleeding hands – to come and help Him in the painful and laborious task of saving their fellows.*

And what seemed to me most passing strange was that those on the platform to whom He called, who heard His voice and felt they ought to obey it – at least, they said they did – those who loved Him much and were in full sympathy with Him in the task He had undertaken – who worshipped Him, or who professed to do so – were so taken up with thier trades and professions and moneysaving and pleasures, and families and circles, and religions and arguments about it, and preparations for going to the mainland that they did not attend to the cry that came to them from this wonderful Being who had Himself gone down into the sea. Anyway, if they heard it they did not heed it – they did not care – and so the multitude went on struggling and shrieking and drowning in the darkness.

Then I saw something that seemed to me stranger than anything that had gone before in this strange vision. I saw that some of these people on the platform, whom this wonderful Being wanted to come and help Him in His difficult task, were always praying and crying to Him to come to them.

Some wanted Him to come and stay with them and spend His time and strength in making them happier. Others wanted Him to come and take away various doubts and misgivings they had respecting the truth of some letters He had written them.

Some wanted Him to come and make them feel more secure on the rock – so secure that they would be quite sure they should never slip off again. Numbers of others wanted Him to make them feel quite certain that they would really get on to the mainland some day because, as a matter of fact, it was well known that some had walked so carelessly as to miss their footing and had fallen back again into the stormy waters.

These people used to meet and get as high up the rock as they could; and looking toward the mainland, where they thought the Great Being was, they would cry out, "Come to us! Come and help us!" And all this time He was down among the poor, struggling, drowning creatures in the angry deep, with His arms around them, trying to drag them out, and looking up – oh! So longingly, but all in vain – to those on the rock, crying to them, with His voice all hoarse with calling, "Come to Me! Come and help Me!"

And then I understood it all. It was plain enough. That sea was the ocean of life – the sea of real, actual, human existence. That lightning was the gleaming of piercing truth coming from Jehovah's Throne. That thunder was the distant echoing of the wrath of God. Those multitudes of people shrieking, struggling, agonizing in the stormy sea were the thousands and thousands of poor harlots and harlot-makers, drunkards and drunkard makers, thieves and liars and blasphemers and ungodly people of every kindred and tongue and nation."[2]

10. What revelation do you have?

Who hath believed our report? And TO WHOM IS THE ARM OF THE LORD REVEALED?

Isaiah 53:1

Who has a revelation? Whom has God given a revelation to? What revelation do you have? Through the Holy Spirit, I have received revelations about the anointing, revelations about shepherding, revelations about church growth, revelations about lay people and the ministry, revelations about loyalty and revelations about leadership. It is on the basis of these revelations that my ministry is birthed.

This is why it is important to pray for the spirit of revelation. The more you pray for the spirit of revelation, the more you pray for your ministry to be birthed! The more you pray for the spirit of revelation, the more you pray for your ministry to be established! Perhaps that is the most important prayer topic you could ever pray – for the spirit of revelation and wisdom! "That the God of our Lord Jesus Christ, the Father of glory, may give unto you the spirit of wisdom and revelation in the knowledge of him" (Ephesians 1:17).

The Secret of Lukewarmness

I know thy works, that thou art neither cold nor hot: I would thou wert cold or hot. So then because THOU ART LUKEWARM, and neither cold nor hot, I WILL SPUE THEE OUT of my mouth.

Because thou sayest, I am RICH, and INCREASED with goods, and have NEED OF NOTHING; and knowest not that thou art wretched, and miserable, and poor, and blind, and naked: I counsel thee to buy of me gold tried in the fire, that thou mayest be rich; and white raiment, that thou mayest be clothed, and that the shame of thy nakedness do not appear; and anoint thine eyes with eyesalve, that thou mayest see.

Revelation 3:15-18

I t is not possible to be a good Christian and not be zealous, faith filled and fiery. Faith by its very nature makes you radical in this world of apathy towards God.

Lukewarmness is the deadly enemy of the church. You must not let the fire of God wane by drifting from His presence. The zeal you have in your heart must be maintained. You must be set on fire by the love that you have for God. Lukewarmness is an ultimate curse that destroys the church and the foundations of Christianity.

1.   God is not deceived by lukewarmness:

...I will SPUE THEE OUT of my mouth.

Revelation 3:16

God is not deceived by lukewarmness! God has no time for lukewarmness! God will spit out lukewarmness. God is not deceived by the false presentation of lukewarmness. Lukewarmness is a mysterious evil, not easily diagnosed for what it really is. The book of Revelation clearly reveals and unveils things that are hidden from open view. Things that are not public knowledge are made known to us if we care to accept them.

Revelation means to unveil and to show something that is hidden.

Dealing with lukewarmness requires great wisdom and great understanding. Most people do not understand God's reaction to lukewarmness. God's reaction to lukewarm people is to spit them out of His mouth. God's reaction to lukewarmness may seem extreme to you. But it only seems extreme to you because you don't know what it really means.

Lukewarmness is the only thing so disgusting to God that it causes Him to spit you out as something detestable.

Lukewarmness is the same as being complacent and satisfied with far less than you should be. What makes lukewarmness so detestable? Lukewarmness is evil because it contains the ingredients of deception and demon activity.

Your lukewarmness is actually a very strong message. Lukewarmness is a message of rejection! That is why the all-wise God and the all-knowing God, meets lukewarmness with total rejection.

To be lukewarm is to be non-committed towards anything. It is deception because no one is really non-committed or lukewarm. Every one is really committed and zealous about something. *Someone's lukewarmness towards you is a sign of his or her rejection of you.* Your lukewarmness towards God is just a revelation of your rejection of God.

You find some people who are cool and quiet towards you. It's as if they cannot really talk much and they are simply not the chatty type. They keep on giving excuses for their non-communicative behaviour. But don't be deceived! They talk and they chat, but not with you!

It is *you* they do not want to talk to!

It is *you* they have rejected!

It is *you* whose company they are not comfortable with!

It is *you* they have evil thoughts about!

It is *you* they wish to be far from!

Watch out for the lukewarm ones! They have rejected you.

Be careful of quiet, polite people who are so perfect in behaviour and controlled in speech. They are dangerous people. There is nothing real about people who do not show emotion, happiness, sadness or any expressive behaviour. Lukewarm people are telling lies by their behaviour! Be like God and reject lukewarm people in your life. Do not accept people who are not as passionate towards you as you are towards them. What is the point in showing so much love and getting so little feedback from the one you love so dearly? Stop believing the excuses of the lukewarm person!

2.   There is self-righteousness in lukewarmness:

For do I now persuade men, or God? or do I SEEK TO PLEASE MEN? for if I yet pleased men, I should not be the servant of Christ.

Galatians 1:10

People who are neither here nor there are often the most self-righteous people you can find. Such people always want to look good on the outside. They do not want to do anything to ruffle feathers. They need to look perfect. They need to look organised. They need to look good. They do not want to offend on this side or on that side. But there is nothing like that in real life.

God is not impressed by people who are mocking you with their "niceness". He spits out these average neither-here-nor-there people. Some of the most evil politicians our world has ever seen presented themselves as nice friends of everyone. Watch out for seemingly nice people! Watch out for these wicked politicians who pretend to belong to every religion. They are evil men disguised in cloaks of lukewarmness. Neither hot nor cold! Neither fully a Christian nor a non-Christian!

God is not impressed by nice people. He is impressed by obedient, humble people who do not mind the mockery of the world. Jesus is looking for people who are ready to withstand the pressure that comes from hearing those mocking words, "He saved others, let him save himself".

Lukewarm people are neither committed here nor there. They are not committed to the heat and they are not committed to the cold. They believe in everything and they support everyone. This kind of self-righteousness will not get you anywhere. People may be impressed, but God is not impressed. God is not interested in people who look good to the world. Anyone who tries to please man cannot be a genuine servant of God.

3.   There is enmity in lukewarmness:

He that is not with me is against me...

Matthew 12:30

People who are not with you are actually against you! This is the wisdom that Jesus gave to us. Watch out for lukewarm, half-hearted, double-minded Christians. These lukewarm people, who are neither here nor there, are actually your enemies.

It takes experience and wisdom to see through their self-righteous mask and to know that the lukewarm gentleman sitting in front of you is your enemy. You will often find the good-looking non-committal fellows to be the most hateful people.

4.   Prosperity is the cause of lukewarmness:

Because thou sayest, I am rich, and increased with goods, and have need of nothing...

Revelation 3:17

Lukewarmness is caused by prosperity, abundance, luxury and earthly achievements. Many preachers today promote greed, materialism, money and prosperity. Most preaching today promotes a terrible lust for wealth. This materialism and prosperity is the root of the church's lukewarmness. When the church said to itself, "I am rich and I have need of nothing" it turned into the famous lukewarm church of Laodicea. Almost all churches that have prospered have left the true way of Christ and fallen into complacency. Hardly can you find a rich person who really serves God. Even the rich people in church hardly give anything much to the Lord. Jesus said, "Hardly shall a rich man enter the Kingdom of heaven."

I counsel thee to buy of me gold tried in the fire, that thou mayest be rich; and white raiment, that thou mayest be clothed, and that the shame of thy nakedness do not appear; and anoint thine eyes with eyesalve, that thou mayest see.

Revelation 3:18

29

5.   Buying   gold   tried   with   fire   will   drive   out lukewarmness:

I counsel thee to buy of me gold tried in the fire...

Revelation 3:18

Having the right vision for your life will wipe out the tendency to become lukewarm. Buying gold tried with fire is the key to overcoming lukewarmness. Gold tried in the fire speaks of eternal riches that cannot be burnt when the fires of death appear. It is not easy to lay your hands on real gold that is tried with fire. As you strive to achieve this spiritual goal, you will never be able to fall back into lukewarmness.

Disregarding earthly prosperity and not valuing it as your life's goal, is key to preventing lukewarmness. Maintaining spiritual and biblical goals of reaching out to the world and building the church of God will prevent lukewarmness.

The spiritual goals that God gives us are more difficult to achieve than any earthly-minded goals. Having a house or a car is not an achievement as far as heaven is concerned. Open yourself up to the great and lofty achievements that will last through eternity. Seek rewards that can follow you into heaven. The great advantage of having these eternal goals is that you will never fall back into lukewarmness.

6.   Buying white raiment will drive out lukewarmness:

I counsel thee to buy of me ...white raiment ...

Revelation 3:18

Seeking for white raiment speaks of seeking righteousness and holiness! Until you die, you will never really achieve this goal. You will be forced to rise up and strive for the high standards of white raiment. Wearing white clothes is not as easy as wearing brown or black clothes. When you wear white, you are kept on your toes, trying to stay clean. It is not easy to avoid soiling your white shirt and trousers. It is not easy to keep the spots out.

The quest for true righteousness, humility, holiness and purity will keep you humble and searching until your last day. Buying clothes at Harrods, Macy's and other great shops of our world is a hundred times easier than buying white raiment that can be worn in heaven. When your goals change and become eternal ones, you will definitely not become lukewarm.

7. Seeking the anointing will drive out lukewarmness:

...anoint thine eyes with eyesalve ...

Revelation 3:18

Seeking the anointing is seeking a hard thing. Seek the anointing and you will be forced to be zealous all the time! Seek the anointing so that your eyes will be anointed and you will see great things. You will become a living wonder through the power of the anointing.

The anointing of the Holy Spirit is a mysterious and obscure experience that is worth following after. Elisha set out to find a double portion of the anointing. Elijah could not guarantee that Elisha would ever catch that anointing. He warned that Elisha had asked for a hard thing.

If Elisha had asked for money, he would probably have received it instantly and become lukewarm afterwards. It is easy to become lukewarm after you have achieved your life's goal. Seeking for spiritual things will keep you on your toes! Seeking for God's power will keep you running, fighting and learning. You will have no time for becoming lukewarm.

The Secret in the Sacrifice

And I beheld, and I heard the voice of many angels round about the throne and the beasts and the elders: and the number of them was ten thousand times ten thousand, and thousands of thousands; Saying with a loud voice, WORTHY IS THE LAMB THAT WAS SLAIN TO RECEIVE POWER, AND RICHES, AND WISDOM, AND STRENGTH, AND HONOUR, AND GLORY, AND BLESSING.

Revelation 5:11-12

T

he seven most sought after treasures are generally accepted to be power, riches, wisdom, strength, honour, glory and blessings. These are the rewards given to the Lamb by Almighty God. These are the most treasured gifts that can be given to anyone: *power, riches, wisdom, strength, honour, glory* and *blessings!*

The key that brings these fantastic sought-after blessings is *"being slain"* according to the will of God. You must never reject sacrifices determined by God for you. When you run away from the sacrifice, you are running away from these powerful blessings. Who in his right mind would run away from power, riches, strength, honour, glory and blessings? No one can imagine that the source of all that God gives us is actually the sacrifice.

To throw away sacrifice is to throw away your power and your future riches.

That is why we embrace the cross! That is why the cross is referred to as "that wondrous cross with a wondrous attraction"!

Today, do not run away from the cross! Run towards what God has chosen for you. Heaven will contain the greatest shocks. The last will be first! The nobodies despised by this world's modern Christians will be the first.

Today, many in the church have thrown out the cross. They have inadvertently thrown out the seven greatest treasures that they actually need and want. Let us return to the cross! To be a Christian is to follow the Lord Jesus and to do what He did. Let us press on and allow ourselves to be slain for His purposes! The things I am saying are not earthly wisdom. I am speaking the wisdom of God in a mystery! It is not earthly wisdom which the Bible says is from down below. The wisdom of God is wrapped in mystery, but it is the wisdom that is above all other wisdom.

The great secret to prosperity, power and greatness is the secret of the sacrifice.

The Lamb who was slain is the one who was worthy to receive power!

The Lamb who was slain is the one who was worthy to receive riches!

The Lamb who was slain is the one who was worthy to receive wisdom!

The Lamb who was slain is the one who was worthy to receive strength!

The Lamb who was slain is the one who was worthy to receive honour!

The Lamb who was slain is the one who was worthy to receive glory!

The Lamb who was slain is the one who was worthy to receive blessing!

The wisdom of God is superior to the wisdom of man. The book of Revelation clearly reveals and unveils things that are hidden from open view. Things that are not public knowledge are made known to us if we care to accept them.

Revelation means to unveil and to show something that is hidden.

As far as the heavens are above the earth, so are His ways above our ways. God's wisdom put His only begotten Son on the cross. God's wisdom has made Him worthy of all these riches, power and glory.

God's wisdom is not taught in the classroom. In the classroom you will learn economics, finance, management, accounting and law. These subjects are only human analysis and observations. None of these studies are the sources of greatness, riches and glory. The true source of riches, strength and glory is obedience to God and a readiness to die for His will. Readiness to die for God is your greatest secret to power, wisdom, strength and honour. Do you seek for riches? Let me advise you: labour not to be rich. Instead, seek first the kingdom of God, His will, His wish and His plan. Lay yourself on the altar and accept, yield and flow with His perfect plan for your life. That is the key to power, strength and riches.

If you are expecting to learn economic principles that are taught in universities, you will not find them in this book. You will need to find for yourself, "Accounting Made Easy", "Economics Made Easy" or "Biology Made Easy". The laws of God and the wisdom of God do not have to make sense to you. Just believe in His ultimate power and grace that will be manifested when you are a sacrificial lamb.

There comes a time when it does not matter what you can achieve. There comes a time where what matters is what you can accept, what you can yield to and what you can flow with! Many of us ministers of God are excited to declare the number of things we have done for God. To be great like Jesus is not about what you have done or the number of things you have built. Jesus did not achieve anything per se. He did not build any schools, hospitals or churches. He is great because He accepted the cross! He is great because He yielded to the cross! He is great because He flowed with God's plan! He is great because He allowed Himself to be baptized with the terrible baptism of the cross.

But Jesus answered and said, Ye know not what ye ask. Are ye able to drink of the cup that I shall drink of, and to be baptized with THE BAPTISM THAT I AM BAPTIZED WITH? They say unto him, we are able.

Matthew 20:22

Just like Jesus, the time will come where you will not be concerned about how many people come to your church or how many followers you have. What will matter is how much pressure you can take! What will matter is how much you can accept! What will matter is how much you can yield to! At that point you will be able to ask people, "What have you been through? What have you survived? What baptism have you experienced?"

The Secret of the Little Book

And I saw another MIGHTY ANGEL come down from heaven, clothed with a cloud: and a rainbow was upon his head, and his face was as it were the sun, and his feet as pillars of fire: And HE HAD IN HIS HAND A LITTLE BOOK open: and he set his right foot upon the sea, and his left foot on the earth.

And the voice which I heard from heaven spake unto me again, and said, Go and take the little book which is open in the hand of the angel which standeth upon the sea and upon the earth. And I went unto the angel, and said unto him, give me the little book. And he said unto me, Take it, and eat it up; and it shall make thy belly bitter, but it shall be in thy mouth sweet as honey. And I TOOK THE LITTLE BOOK OUT OF THE ANGEL'S HAND, AND ATE IT UP; and it was in my mouth sweet as honey: and as soon as I had eaten it, my belly was bitter.

And he said unto me, Thou must PROPHESY AGAIN BEFORE MANY PEOPLES, AND NATIONS, AND TONGUES, AND KINGS.

Revelation 10:1-2, 8-11

1.   The little book will determine your future ministry:

Y our entire ministry is determined by the little book that you eat.

The book of Revelation clearly reveals and unveils things that are hidden from open view. Things that are not public knowledge are made known to us if we care to accept them.

Revelation means to unveil and to show something that is hidden.

Few people realise how important and powerful it is to devour God-sent little books. There are several important secrets that are contained in this testimony of the mighty angel with the little book. Again, this is not the wisdom you can learn in a secular school. There is no secular school that will teach you the revelation of the little book. This is wisdom from above. This is the wisdom of God in a mystery. This wisdom is hidden from those who are carnally minded.

2.   The little book and angels:

And the voice which I heard from heaven spake unto me again, and said, Go and take the LITTLE BOOK which is open in the hand of the ANGEL which standeth upon the sea and upon the earth.

Revelation 10:8

Angels are involved in delivering books to you. I have never seen an angel physically put a book into my hand. However, angels are always involved in our lives without our knowing. We are delivered from many evils without even knowing what almost killed us. Many things that happen in our lives are orchestrated by angels.

3.   The little book is the mission of the big angel:

And the voice which I heard from heaven spake unto me again, and said, Go and take the LITTLE BOOK which is open in the hand of the ANGEL WHICH STANDETH UPON THE SEA AND UPON THE EARTH.

Revelation 10:8

It is time to grow up in your understanding of what a book is. It is time for you to value books as much as God does. The largest angel ever sent to the human race brought nothing greater than a little book. This shows us that a book is a very important item. For God to send an angel all the way from heaven with a book shows how important books are. If books are important to God, books must be important to you! You would have thought that the angel of the Lord would do something more powerful and dramatic than delivering a little book. The angel did not even bring a big book. The secret found in a little book can make all the difference in your life and ministry.

4.   Take the little book:

And I went unto the angel, and said unto him, Give me the little book...

Revelation 10:9

It is important to take the books that God has presented to you. Perhaps the book is lying on your table. Perhaps the book is for sale in the bookshop. Perhaps it is the first time you are encountering such a wonderful book. It is important for you to reach out and take the book. I remember a pastor who came in contact with my books. Somebody had given one of my books to him as a gift. He admired them and said some nice things, but he never actually took the books home and studied them. When I met him I could tell that he was in difficulty and needed to really study some of the things I had written about. He simply did not reach out to take the book that God had brought his way.

5.   The little book must be "eaten":

...And he said unto me, Take it, and EAT IT UP; and it shall make thy belly bitter, but it shall be in thy mouth sweet as honey.

Revelation 10:9

"Reading" a book is different from "eating" a book. When you "eat" something and digest it, it becomes a part of you. It is dissolved, digested and absorbed into your very flesh. When you "eat" a book, it completely dissolves, disappears and is absorbed into your flesh. When you have "eaten" a book it becomes a part of you. No one is able to tell where you got your revelation from when you speak. The revelation has become a part of you and when you speak you are speaking of yourself. Most people do not "eat" books. That is why they do not benefit from them. Continuous and repeated reading, combined with studying and referring to the Bible will help you in your quest to "eat" a book. Reading a book over and over and listening to messages on the same subject will help you to digest a book.

6.   The little book will be sweet in your mouth:

...And he said unto me, Take it, and eat it up; and it shall make thy belly bitter, but IT SHALL BE IN THY MOUTH SWEET AS HONEY.

Revelation 10:9

To the making of many books there will be no end. There are simply millions of books that have been produced. It is important therefore to distinguish between the books God has sent to you and the ones you must not waste your time on. A God-sent book will be sweet in your mouth. Do not waste your time on books that are bitter from the word go. As soon as I notice that I struggle to understand the basics in a book, I consider it not to be one of the books God has sent to me through His angel.

When God sends you a book, He makes it palatable, enjoyable and readable. There are books you cannot read because you do not understand them. There are many books I simply do not understand. The books you do not understand are not the books that God has sent to you. Take note of books that are sweet and enjoyable to read.

7.   The little book will be bitter in your belly:

And I took the little book out of the angel's hand, and ate it up; and it was in my mouth sweet as honey: and AS SOON AS I HAD EATEN IT, MY BELLY WAS BITTER.

Revelation 10:10

The true Word of God will not only be sweet. The Word of God and the call of God will always have a bitter component. All of ministry has bitterness embedded within it. There are things that are hard, painful and bitter in ministry. As you soak in the books, it will sound all logical, easy and the most obvious thing to do. But as you go on, deeper into the ministry, there are many bitter and painful experiences you will have to endure because of what you have read.

8.   The little book will launch you into the four dimensions of a greater ministry (people, nations, tongues and kings):

And he said unto me, Thou must prophesy again before many PEOPLES, and NATIONS, and TONGUES, and KINGS.

Revelation 10:11

The dimension of many people: Many ministers do not have a ministry to large numbers of people. Most ministers speak to a small number of people. Most pastors are not privileged to grow to a stage where they minister to thousands. You are receiving that grace right now! Through the little book, you will be launched into the realm of preaching to thousands.

Do you want to speak to many people?

Do you want your church to grow?

Do you want to graduate from speaking to little fellowships?

There was a time in my life I only spoke to small groups and little fellowships that could sit around in a circle. God sent His power into my life through a little book written by Kenneth Hagin. Today, I speak to many people by the grace of God.

The dimension of many tongues: Most preachers preach in their own language. Today, God is launching you into a realm where you will speak to other languages. That is a promotion! I used to hate having interpreters. I felt that interpreters slowed me down. When I discovered this scripture, I realised that it was a promotion that I needed so many interpreters. God was taking me higher to the place where I constantly needed an interpreter because I constantly had "other tongues" sitting in front of me. Do you want to preach with an interpreter? Do you want to preach to people of other tongues? It is time to "soak in" the little book! It's time to eat it up. Through a little book, you will be launched into a higher dimension of ministry.

The dimension of many nations: Most preachers never travel outside their home country. Again, it takes the special grace of God to be able to preach in other nations.

One day, I was invited to another country to preach the Word of God. When I arrived, I was put in a room without windows. One of my travelling companions asked me, "Why do you come to this place where they put you in a room without windows?"

I asked him, "Have you ever been invited to another country to preach?"

He said, "No, I have never been invited to another country to preach."

Then I told him, "It is a great privilege for anyone to invite you to preach anywhere."

It is an even greater privilege to be invited to another country to preach. It takes the great power of God for you to be invited to another nation. Such things only happen to people who have eaten the little books.

Do you want to be invited to other nations? I'm sure you do! God wants to send you to other nations. Your ministry will not be complete until you go to other nations. A prophet is not accepted in his own home. Eat the little book that God has presented to you and you will be on the next flight to the nations. When you are in the nations, you will be accepted as a great prophet. You will be surprised at the grace of God that will be manifested when you minister.

The dimension of speaking to kings: Do you want to speak to kings? Most pastors will never speak to a king. The "king" represents the president, the prime minister, the mayor, the chief or any secularly important person in your city. God is going to lift you up until all such people pay attention to you! How will this come about? It will come about when you eat, digest, soak in, absorb, study and receive the little books that God is sending to you by His angel. Through the little books you will receive great wisdom, and kings will seek to hear your opinion.

The Secrets of Death

And I saw when the Lamb opened one of the seals, and I heard, as it were the noise of thunder, one of the four beasts saying, Come and see. And I saw, and behold a white horse: and he that sat on him had a bow; and a crown was given unto him: and he went forth conquering, and to conquer.

And when he had opened the second seal, I heard the second beast say, Come and see. And there went out another horse that was red: and power was given to him that sat thereon to take peace from the earth, and that they should kill one another: and there was given unto him a great sword.

And when he had opened the third seal, I heard the third beast say, Come and see. And I beheld, and lo a black horse; and he that sat on him had a pair of balances in his hand. And I heard a voice in the midst of the four beasts say, A measure of wheat for a penny, and three measures of barley for a penny; and see thou hurt not the oil and the wine. And when he had opened the fourth seal, I heard the voice of the fourth beast say, Come and see. AND I LOOKED, AND BEHOLD A PALE HORSE: AND HIS NAME THAT SAT ON HIM

WAS DEATH, and Hell followed with him. And power was given unto them over the fourth part of the earth, to kill with sword, and with hunger, and with death, and with the beasts of the earth.

Revelation 6:1-8

Death is one of the greatest moments in a Christian's life. It is a moment we all dread but will have to face anyway. Most people do not think about death at all. Unspiritual people do not think of death at all. Most ministers of the gospel consider death to be a very negative thing that should not be discussed. However, there are many secrets hidden in the reality of death.

The book of Revelation clearly reveals and unveils things that are hidden from open view. Things that are not public knowledge are made known to us if we care to accept them.

Revelation means to unveil and to show something that is hidden.

Let's look at the revelation of the secrets of death.

1. The revelation: Death happens first in the spirit realm.

And I looked, and behold a pale horse: and his name that sat on him was Death, and Hell followed with him. And power was given unto them over the fourth part of the earth, to kill with sword, and with hunger, and with death, and with the beasts of the earth.

Revelation 6:8

Many people are dead long before they actually die physically because the move towards death has already taken place in the spirit. It is important that you view death in a very spiritual way.

Death is a deeply spiritual event. As you can see in the scripture above, long before a whole lot of people died, a pale horse with a rider called death had been released to gallop through the heavens. Through this spiritual event, by means of this spiritual horse, a quarter of the people on earth were killed by hunger, death and wild animals.

God has given us spiritual power. And what are we doing with this power? Many things have a spiritual origin. Death equally has a spiritual origin! The scripture above shows us that death occurred when a spiritual horse with a spiritual rider went out riding. Since death is such a spiritual event involving spiritual horses and spiritual riders, it is possible to block it, challenge it, delay it or fight it in the spirit realm. In other words, you can use your spiritual power to pray about death when it is coming for you. You do not have to die before your time.

2. The revelation: Death involves a weighty decision in Heaven.

Precious in the sight of the Lord is the death of his saints.

Psalm 116:15

The death of a saint is truly a precious and weighty decision that God has to make. Never think that God's servants are whimsically removed from this earth. For you to die, God will have to take an important decision. John the Baptist who was declared to be the greatest man born of women did not die because of some whimsical decision of a jealous and wicked woman. No, no, no! John the Baptist died because of a weighty decision that was taken in Heaven. The angels were asked to stand back as God's honoured servant was withdrawn from the earth. Do you think that Jesus Christ was killed on the cross by the wickedness of jealous Pharisees? Certainly not! The death of Jesus was something that was planned thousands of years ago. Precious in the eyes of the Lord is the death of His saints.

3. The revelation: Death is a spiritual appointment.

And he spake a parable unto them, saying, the ground of a certain rich man brought forth plentifully: And he thought within himself, saying, what shall I do, because I have no room where to bestow my fruits? And he said, This will I do: I will pull down my barns, and build greater; and there will I bestow all my fruits and my goods.

And I will say to my soul, Soul, thou hast much goods laid up for many years; take thine ease, eat, drink, and be merry.

But GOD SAID unto him, thou fool, THIS NIGHT THY SOUL SHALL BE REQUIRED OF THEE: then whose shall those things be, which thou hast provided?

Luke 12:16-20

It is indeed appointed once for men to die (Hebrews 9:27). But when is that appointment going to take place? It is going to take place on the day that has been determined by God. The rich fool did not realise that a decision had been taken in the heavens for his withdrawal from the earth. When God takes a decision about having a meeting with you, you will have no choice but to keep the appointment.

You cannot live beyond the day that you have been appointed to die. The boundaries have been appointed and no amount of precautions or preventive measures can stop death or move that boundary. "Seeing his days are determined, the number of his months are with thee, thou hast appointed his bounds that he cannot pass" (Job 14:5).

4. There are two types of death: the death of the righteous and the death of the wicked.

...Let me die THE DEATH OF THE RIGHTEOUS, and let my last end be like his!

Numbers 23:10

Say unto them, As I live, saith the Lord God, I have no pleasure in THE DEATH OF THE WICKED; but that the wicked turn from his way and live: turn ye, turn ye from your evil ways; for why will ye die, O house of Israel?

Ezekiel 33:11

The death of the righteous and the death of the wicked are the two types of deaths that exist. These are two completely different experiences. The prayer is clear: "Let me die the death of a righteous man". The death of a righteous man is a good experience but the death of a wicked man is a terrible experience filled with torment and fear.

5. The death of the righteous is a blessing:

And I heard a voice from heaven saying unto me, Write, BLESSED ARE THE DEAD WHICH DIE IN THE LORD from henceforth: Yea, saith the Spirit, that they may rest from their labours; and their works do follow them.

Revelation 14:13

Death is a blessing to those who are in the Lord. "Blessed are the dead who die in the Lord". The Word of God is clear. It is a blessing to be dead if you die in the Lord.

6. The death of the righteous is gain:

For to me to live is Christ, and to die is gain.

Philippians 1:21

Death, for a Christian, is gain. Gain means advancement, improvement, advantage, increase, addition, profit, reward and benefit. Death, to the righteous, is to achieve advancement, advantage, increase, addition, profit, reward and benefit. It is time to believe the Word of God about what death really is to a believer. Death is gain! To die is gain!

The Secret of the Olive Tree and the Candlestick

And there was given me a reed like unto a rod: and the angel stood, saying, Rise, and measure the temple of God, and the altar, and them that worship therein. But the court which is without the temple leave out, and measure it not; for it is given unto the Gentiles: and the holy city shall they tread under foot forty and two months. And I will give power unto MY TWO WITNESSES, and they shall prophesy a thousand two hundred and threescore days, clothed in sackcloth.

THESE ARE THE TWO OLIVE TREES, AND THE TWO CANDLESTICKS STANDING BEFORE THE GOD OF THE EARTH. And if any man will hurt them, fire proceedeth out of their mouth, and devoureth their enemies: and if any man will hurt them, he must in this manner be killed.

THESE HAVE POWER to shut heaven, that it rain not in the days of their prophecy: and have power over waters to turn them to blood, and to smite the earth with all plagues, as often as they will.

Revelation 11:1-6

The secret of the olive tree and the candlestick is a revelation of what it means to be a perfect minister of the gospel. The two famous prophets who would minister for one thousand two hundred and sixty days were called the olive trees and the candlesticks of the Lord. These amazing prophets would be killed and rise from the dead in the full view of the whole world.

These prophets give us the picture of what a really anointed minister can and should be. The two high-powered ministers of revelation were described as being both olive trees and candlesticks. Their descriptions as olive trees and candlesticks give us the vision of what we must attain to.

This twofold description of God's servant is the description you must aim at achieving for yourself. A perfect minister has two completely different parts to him. The olive tree part of him and the candle stick part of him. One side is always receiving and one side is always giving.

What It Means to be an Olive Tree

When a minister is an olive tree, he is constantly being watered. Without being constantly watered by the Word, a minister soon becomes empty and has nothing to say.

When a minister is an olive tree, he is constantly being nourished. A minister must constantly hear the Word of God and be blessed by it. He must constantly read the Word of God and be blessed by it.

A child once made a comment to me. She said, "My parents, who are pastors only read the Bible when they are going to preach. Apart from that, they never read the Bible." That is not a good example of an olive tree. An olive tree is constantly receiving. An olive tree minister does not only receive the Word of God when he is going to minister.

When a minister is an olive tree, he is constantly growing and developing. So sad it is, to see ministers who have stopped growing and developing. In all my travels, one of the tragedies I have observed is the lack of drive or vision in some pastors. When they have a car and a house they feel they have reached their peak in ministry. They then begin to die and stay in one place.

When a minister is an olive tree, he is constantly being beaten to produce fruit. Olive trees are beaten with sticks to make the olives drop off.

When THOU BEATEST THINE OLIVE TREE, thou shalt not go over the boughs again: it shall be for the stranger, for the fatherless, and for the widow.

Deuteronomy 24:20

A real minister who is an olive tree is constantly under fire and persecution. That is the life of a true minister. There is no need to complain about your many troubles if you are in the ministry. That is the portion of an olive tree! Your portion is to be beaten so that the fruits can fall off! Most of the powerful messages, books and fruits I have borne have come from my troubles and beatings in ministry. Without these beatings I simply wouldn't have had any insight into the realities that I have to minister about.

When a minister is an olive tree, he is constantly bearing fruit. The olive tree is continually being shaken for the fruits to fall off.

When thus it shall be in the midst of the land among the people, there shall be as THE SHAKING OF AN OLIVE TREE, and as the gleaning grapes when the vintage is done.

Isaiah 24:13

Bearing fruit is the sign that you are a living olive tree. Olive trees are some of the oldest trees living today. The olive trees in the Garden of Gethsemane are said to be two thousand years old. I once met a seventy-nine year old minister preaching at a convention. There was no sign of his strength or health abating. His preaching was powerful and life changing. He sounded nicer and better than we the younger ones. That is a real olive tree; very old but still around and competing with the younger arrogant trees for space and fruit bearing.

What it Means to be a Candlestick

When a minister is a candlestick, he is burning the oil and producing light. This means that he is using the anointing God has given him to shine the light of God.

When a minister is a candlestick, he is constantly shining the light of God and bringing light and hope to the people. To live under the anointing and to shine the light of God's power and presence is an awesome thing. To experience fellowship with a candlestick of the Lord is simply awesome.

A candlestick is a person who is shining. A candlestick is very much affected by the oil it has within it. A candlestick is someone who loves the Lord and lives in the presence of God. Simple conversations with a "candlestick" turn into amazing and anointed sessions in the tangible presence of God.

Develop yourself into one of God's wonderful candlesticks; where you are always using and enjoying the anointing and presence of God!

... fervent in spirit; serving the Lord;

Romans 12:11

VICTORY SECRET NO.8

The Secret of Defeat

And there was given me a reed like unto a rod: and the angel stood, saying, Rise, and measure the temple of God, and the altar, and them that worship therein. But the court which is without the temple leave out, and measure it not; for it is given unto the Gentiles: and the holy city shall they tread under foot forty and two months.

And I will give power unto MY TWO WITNESSES, AND THEY SHALL PROPHESY A THOUSAND TWO HUNDRED AND THREESCORE DAYS, clothed in sackcloth.

These are the two olive trees, and the two candlesticks standing before the God of the earth. And if any man will hurt them, fire proceedeth out of their mouth, and devoureth their enemies: and if any man will hurt them, he must in this manner be killed.

These have power to shut heaven, that it rain not in the days of their prophecy: and have power over waters to turn them to blood, and to smite the earth with all plagues, as often as they will.

And WHEN THEY SHALL HAVE FINISHED their testimony, THE BEAST that ascendeth out of the bottomless pit shall make war against them, and

SHALL OVERCOME THEM, AND KILL THEM. And their dead bodies shall lie in the street of the great city, which spiritually is called Sodom and Egypt, where also our Lord was crucified.

And they of the people and kindreds and tongues and **NATIONS SHALL SEE THEIR DEAD BODIES** three days and an half, and shall not suffer their dead bodies to be put in graves. And they that dwell upon the earth shall rejoice over them, and make merry, and shall send gifts one to another; because these two prophets tormented them that dwelt on the earth.

Revelation 11:1-10

1. God has predetermined both victory and defeat.

Victory is a deeply spiritual event. Defeat is also a highly spiritual event. The two witnesses in the book of Revelation are wonderful ministers of God. Their lives and ministries give us the four secrets of the predetermined lives of ministers of the gospel.

The book of Revelation clearly reveals and unveils things that are hidden from open view. Things that are not public knowledge are made known to us if we care to accept them.

Revelation means to unveil and to show something that is hidden.

Understanding the things that are determined will give you a great sense of peace as you serve God. Understanding that God is a God of predestination is important so that you do not become anxious. There are stresses, persecutions, difficulties and even defeats that God has determined for you to go through.

The Word of God teaches us that God rules in the affairs of men. You must believe that He is ruling and determining events that are happening in your life. Mysteriously, God has a hand in whatever seems to be a defeat in your life. Modern Christians do not understand how God can have a hand in their apparent defeat.

And he was driven from the sons of men; and his heart was made like the beasts, and his dwelling was with the wild asses: they fed him with grass like oxen, and his body was wet with the dew of heaven; till he knew that THE MOST HIGH GOD RULED IN THE KINGDOM OF MEN, and that he appointeth over it whomsoever he will.

Daniel 5:21

2. You may have to accept defeat when it is God's will.

It was the will of God for the two witnesses to be overcome. This is a great secret that will not be understood by people who are fixated in earthly logic. When Jesus said, "He who loses his life will gain it", He defied the logical thinking of many people. Earthly logic says, "win-win-win, succeed-succeed-succeed". There are greater victories that are achieved by losing and accepting defeat when it is God's will.

Most prophets love to predict good news. Sometimes, God does not give the good news that we want to hear. Bible prophets never spoke only good things. Today, it is profitable to prophesy good things to itching ears. Every "good news" prophecy earns a higher salary than a "bad news" prophecy.

The true prophet, Jeremiah, did not predict good news. He prophesied doom, destruction and captivity. He was a genuine prophet. He told them it would take more than seventy years for things to change. In other words, the change would come after their lifetime. Jeremiah encouraged the people to plant gardens, to build houses and seek the peace of the city He had placed them in.

For thus saith the Lord of hosts, the God of Israel; Let not your prophets and your diviners, that be in the midst of you, deceive you, neither hearken to your dreams which ye cause to be dreamed. For they prophesy falsely unto you in my name: I have not sent them, saith the Lord.

For thus saith the Lord, that after seventy years be accomplished at Babylon I will visit you, and perform my good word toward you, in causing you to return to this place. For I know the thoughts that I think toward you, saith the Lord, thoughts of peace, and not of evil, to give you an expected end.

Jeremiah 29:8-11

3. **You cannot be defeated until you have finished your work.**

It was actually because the two ministers had completed their mission that they were defeated. Every aspect of your ministry will be successful until you finish your work. The cars will work, the planes will work, the buses will work, the rockets will work and the computers will work successfully until the day your mission is completed. However, when the mission is over, many things that worked will no longer work.

You will not and you cannot be overcome until it is over. Being defeated may be the mysterious will of God for you. When you finish your work, you may meet things that have mysteriously been given the power to overcome and defeat you. You may be perplexed because you have been so successful in everything you have done in the past. When you encounter certain defeats, you must seek the Lord to know what is happening. It may be time to turn to Him that "smiteth" you.

For the people TURNETH NOT UNTO HIM THAT SMITETH THEM, neither do they seek the Lord of hosts.

Isaiah 9:13

4. The end only comes when you have finished your testimony.

Do not worry about the end. It is God's will for you to finish your calling and run your race. It is only when you have no more usefulness on this earth that the end will come.

The two witnesses were successful until they completed their mission. We often feel sorry for men of God when it seems they have died too early. Often, such people have finished their calling and it is better that they are withdrawn from the earth. John the Baptist had a special role of preparing the way of the Lord. His mission was not to live long or build several houses. His mission was to prepare the way of the Lord. Once Jesus was in place, he genuinely had no reason to continue living on this earth. John the Baptist was extracted because his mission was over. It may have looked like defeat but it was a spiritual extraction. Today, extractions are going on all over the world.

The Secret of God's Disguises

I was in the Spirit on the Lord's day, and heard behind me a great voice, as of a trumpet, Saying, I am Alpha and Omega, the first and the last: and, What thou seest, write in a book, and send it unto the seven churches which are in Asia; unto Ephesus, and unto Smyrna, and unto Pergamos, and unto Thyatira, and unto Sardis, and unto Philadelphia, and unto Laodicea.

And I turned to see the voice that spake with me. And being turned, I saw seven golden candlesticks; and in the midst of the seven candlesticks one like unto THE SON OF MAN, clothed with a garment down to the foot, and girt about the paps with a golden girdle.

HIS HEAD AND HIS HAIRS WERE WHITE LIKE WOOL, AS WHITE AS SNOW; AND HIS EYES WERE AS A FLAME OF FIRE; AND HIS FEET LIKE UNTO FINE BRASS, AS IF THEY BURNED IN A FURNACE; AND HIS VOICE AS THE SOUND OF MANY WATERS.

And he had in his right hand seven stars: and out of his mouth went a sharp twoedged sword: and HIS

COUNTENANCE WAS AS THE SUN SHINETH IN HIS STRENGTH.

And when I saw him, I fell at his feet as dead. And he laid his right hand upon me, saying unto me, Fear not; I am the first and the last: I am he that liveth, and was dead; and, behold, I am alive for evermore, Amen; and have the keys of hell and of death.

Revelation 1:10-18

Years ago, I heard about how Saddam Hussein would move around without being noticed. A convoy of Mercedes Benz cars would pass and everyone would think he was in one of them. He would then arrive alone in a taxi. At times he would come in an ambulance. Indeed, many heads of state successfully disguise themselves.

Jesus Christ came to this world completely disguised and hidden from the wicked men of this earth. The book of Revelation reveals that Jesus Christ was completely disguised when He walked on this earth.

The book of Revelation clearly reveals and unveils things that are hidden from open view. Things that are not public knowledge are made known to us if we care to accept them.

Revelation means to unveil and to show something that is hidden.

Jesus Christ is revealed in the book of Revelation: His head is white as wool. His eyes are flaming fire. His feet are like burning brass and His voice is like the sound of water. Amazing! In reality, this picture is who and what Jesus Christ is: His glistening face, His piercing eyes, His wonderful voice, His burning feet, His powerful mouth and His glorious hair. Wow! So this is who He really was!

But when He walked amongst us by the Sea of Galilee, He had none of these features. Jesus had put on a remarkable disguise and walked amongst us in humility and weakness, allowing only God-fearing people to recognize Him.

What an amazing disguise God wore as He walked amongst us! That is scary! So what other disguises does He have today? Does He still walk amongst us without us knowing? Indeed He does! He is walking amongst us with perfect disguises. Most of us hardly recognize Jesus when He is around. His disguises are simply too amazing.

Perhaps, Jesus Christ should be given the highest award for the most outstanding disguises of all time. In Matthew 25, we see an array of disguises He uses. Let us go through some of the disguises that Jesus is using today. Knowing these disguises is important, because it helps us to know when we may be inadvertently dealing with Jesus Christ.

Woe unto to you if you miss these disguises and mishandle the Son of God!

The Disguises of Jesus

1. The disguise of a hungry and thirsty person.

For I was an HUNGRED, and ye gave me no meat: I was THIRSTY, and ye gave me no drink:

Matthew 25:42

2. The disguise of a homeless person.

I was a STRANGER, and ye took me not in: naked, and ye clothed me not: sick, and in prison, and ye visited me not.

Matthew 25:43

3. The disguise of a naked person.

I was a stranger, and ye took me not in: NAKED, and ye clothed me not: sick, and in prison, and ye visited me not.

Matthew 25:43

4. The disguise of a sick person.

I was a stranger, and ye took me not in: naked, and ye clothed me not: SICK, and in prison, and ye visited me not.

Matthew 25:43

5.   The disguise of a prisoner.

I was a stranger, and ye took me not in: naked, and ye clothed me not: sick, and IN PRISON, and ye visited me not.

Matthew 25:43

Disguises of a Man of God

We must also realize that God has given men of God disguises that they cannot shake off. Do not be disturbed if the world does not recognize you in your disguise. They are not supposed to recognize you.

Do you want to know more about your God-given disguise? I am sure you do. Your disguise will make you look humble and lowly. All the disguises of Jesus made Him look very humble and lowly. God gives His servants disguises. These disguises make the servant of God look weak, humble and powerless.

Think about it. God was born in a stable! God grew up as a carpenter! God was crucified as a criminal! But look at Jesus in Heaven. How glorious! How marvellous! The Jesus who came to this earth in this humble form is seen in the book of Revelation in His true and glorious state.

What looks great on this earth will not look great in Heaven. Jesus is the best example of this because God has chosen the weak things of this world to confound the mighty. Your greatness is not determined by how you appear on earth. God has intentionally given you things that give you a humble appearance.

The reason why the cross is the power of God unto salvation is because it was the most humble thing that God gave to Christ to bear. As you go higher in the Lord, He will give you things that make you lowly and humble. Ask yourself a question: What is it that breaks you down? What is it that makes you cry? What is it that humbles you? What is it that makes you lower than other human beings? What is it that makes you less than your friends and colleagues?

Anything that makes you "inferior" or "less" is part of that humble cloak given to you by the Lord. It is your cross! It will be exchanged for glory one day. Our light affliction works out for us an eternal weight of glory (2 Corinthians 4:17).

Your humble cloak may be your skin colour, your nationality, your level of education, your family background, your peculiar circumstance, your poverty, some peculiar physical defect, your failed marriage, your failed home, your failed ministry, your failed children, your broken heart, your failed business, your failed exam, your sickness, the death of a loved one or any other disappointment of your life.

Do not be deceived by the humble things that God has put on your lap. God has decided to give many great ministers humble appearances on earth. Receive the wisdom that Paul had and embrace the things that make you weak. Have a proper respect for things that place a reproach, a necessity and a distressing situation on you.

Do not be deceived by the lowly appearance of people on earth. You may be dealing with someone who will be a glorious and honoured king in Heaven.

Do not be misled or do not misread the things that make you humble on this earth. God allows humbling things to happen to you and to be with you. However, when you appear in Heaven you will be shining and glorious.

God Has Chosen Lowly Disguises

1. **The disguise of foolish things:** "But God hath chosen the foolish things of the world to confound the wise; and God hath chosen the weak things of the world to confound the things which are mighty; and base things of the world, and things which are despised, hath God chosen, yea, and things which are not, to bring to nought things that are: that no flesh should glory in his presence."

   1 Corinthians 1:27-29

2. **The disguise of lightly esteemed things:** "... for that which is highly esteemed among men is abomination in the sight of God."

Luke 16:15

3. **The disguise of being last:** "And he sat down, and called the twelve, and saith unto them, If any man desire to be first, the same shall be last of all, and servant of all."

Mark 9:35

4. **The disguise of being a servant:** "But he that is greatest among you shall be your servant."

Matthew 23:11

5. **The disguise of infirmities:** "And he said unto me, My grace is sufficient for thee: for my strength is made perfect in weakness. Most gladly therefore will I rather glory in my infirmities, that the power of Christ may rest upon me."

2 Corinthians 12:9

6. **The disguise of earthen vessels:** "But we have this treasure in earthen vessels, that the excellency of the power may be of God, and not of us."

2 Corinthians 4:7

7. **The disguise of afflictions:** "For our light affliction, which is but for a moment, worketh for us a far more exceeding and eternal weight of glory; while we look not at the things which are seen, but at the things which are not seen: for the things which are seen are temporal; but the things which are not seen are eternal."

2 Corinthians 4:17-18

VICTORY SECRET NO.10

The Secret of the Mark of the Beast

And I beheld another beast coming up out of the earth; and he had two horns like a lamb, and he spake as a dragon. And he exerciseth all the power of the first beast before him, and causeth the earth and them which dwell therein to worship the first beast, whose deadly wound was healed. And he doeth great wonders, so that he maketh fire come down from heaven on the earth in the sight of men, And deceiveth them that dwell on the earth by the means of those miracles which he had power to do in the sight of the beast; saying to them that dwell on the earth, that they should make an image to the beast, which had the wound by a sword, and did live. And he had power to give life unto the image of the beast, that the image of the beast should both speak, and cause that as many as would not worship the image of the beast should be killed. And HE CAUSETH ALL, BOTH SMALL AND GREAT, RICH AND POOR, FREE AND BOND, TO RECEIVE A MARK in their right hand, or in their foreheads: and that no man might buy or sell, save he that had THE MARK, or the name of the beast, or the number of his name.

Revelation 13:11-17

The mark of business and profitability is the mark of the beast. Without this mark, no one will be able to buy or sell. Therefore the mark of the beast is the mark of doing business and making profit.

The mark of the beast is to be placed on the right hand and on the forehead. The mark of the beast on the forehead results in your mind and thinking being dominated in every activity, by whether or not you will make profit. The mark of the beast on your right hand simply means that the mark of business and profitability will affect all the works of your hands. The mark of the beast releases utter corruption into anything it touches.

When the mark of business and profitability is on something, it will always be run as a business. In the secular world, things that are dominated by profit are usually corrupted. When politicians are corrupted by the mark of the beast, they run the nation as their personal business, seeking to get as much for themselves as they can.

When medical doctors are influenced solely by making profit, their practice is corrupted. For instance a doctor may choose to do a Caesarean section because he would make more money from that, than from a normal delivery. When lawyers seek only to make profit rather than doing what is right, they sacrifice their conscience and defend the indefensible.

The desire for more and more money always corrupts and destroys. The mark of the beast is the ultimate corrupter and destroyer!

Today, many churches and ministries have the mark of profit making. The book of Revelation clearly reveals and unveils things that are hidden from open view. Things that are not public knowledge are made known to us if we care to accept them.

Revelation means to unveil and to show something that is hidden.

In this case, the revelation of our corruption is plain to see. Everything is for sale! People work in the church because it is a good job and they will earn a high salary. Many people who do ministry are profit oriented and money conscious. They will say, "I have to live off my work."

However, in real ministry, you cannot have this mark. If you have this mark of profitability on your ministry, you will attract the wrath of God instead of the anointing of the Holy Spirit. This mark is so detestable to God that it is referred to over and over as the basis for God's judgment and wrath.

And the smoke of their torment ascendeth up for ever and ever: and they have no rest day nor night, who worship the beast and his image, and whosoever receiveth THE MARK of his name.

Revelation 14:11

There is a good reason for God's dislike and utter rejection of this mark of the beast. Through the mark of the beast, ministry experiences a sharp decline.

Ask yourself, "How much of God's work can be done by looking at profitability?" "How many crusades can be held by looking at profitability?" The mark of the beast makes you calculate what you will get out of something - "How much am I going to make?" "Will I break even?"

With this mark of profitability, business and trade, you cannot plant churches in poor towns and villages. There are not enough rich cities where a church can make enough money to be profitable. Most places that need to have churches planted in them will not be profitable financially.

With this mark of profitability, business and trade, you cannot have crusades in certain nations' cities, towns or villages because it will simply not be profitable! There will not be enough money to pay for the crusade. Much soul winning will therefore be prevented because it is not profitable financially. Have you ever wondered why there are so few evangelists?

Much of the church has this mark today; much of the church only does things that are profitable financially. The result of this mark is a sharp decline in evangelism and church planting.

Writing and publishing spiritual books with genuine messages from God has been completely set aside because of the mark of the beast. The fact that a book has to be profitable means that the truth cannot be published anymore! The reality is that truth is not popular! Many of the books available today are simply products of the profit making industry that has decided what has to be written.

I remember when a man of God was sued by a publisher for getting divorced. The publishers were upset because people would not buy enough of a divorced pastor's books. This man of God had already been paid in advance to write a particular book. The money-making publishers had their eyes glued on the profits they could make from the man of God's writings. Because the man of God was divorced, the publishers felt that fewer people would buy the books. The eyes of the publishers are not on the message, but on the money!

I wrote a book entitled, *"Losing, Suffering, Sacrificing and Dying."* An American publisher reacted to my book at a book fair and declared that it was the worst book title she had ever seen. She also said that no one would buy it. What she did not realize was that my book was not written for profit or popularity. That book contains the truth about the cross of Jesus. I don't have any money-making publisher who tells me what I can write. I can write whatever God gives me to write!

I could not have been in full time ministry if I was thinking of profitability. I was a doctor with a bright future ahead of me. I could never have taken the decision to work for God if I was thinking of getting money and making profit.

Is the work of your hand tainted with this detestable mark of the beast? Is everything you do affected by your desire to make profit? If you take decisions based on business and profitability, then you have the detestable mark of the beast!

And the third angel followed them, saying with a loud voice, If any man worship the beast and his image, and receive his mark in his FOREHEAD, or in his HAND,

Revelation 14:9

When the mark of the beast is on your head, all your thoughts, plans, purposes, ideas and motives are tainted by this terrible mark.

When the mark of the beast is on your hand, all your activities, actions, programs, jobs and work are tainted by this terrible and evil sign.

And the third angel followed them, saying with a loud voice, If any man worship the beast and his image, and receive his mark in his forehead, or in his hand, The same shall drink of the wine of the wrath of God, which is poured out without mixture into the cup of his indignation; and he shall be tormented with fire and brimstone in the presence of the holy angels, and in the presence of the Lamb:

Revelation 14:9-10

Profiteering, marketing, buying, selling, trading must not mark and taint your ministry. You will receive the judgment of God on your ministry when you have that mark. It is important to overcome not only the beast himself but also the mark of being profit-oriented in everything.

There will definitely be ministries that will not be affected by this mark. They will remain pure and unaffected by the spirit of profiteering, marketing trading and money-making. The book of Revelation predicts that some people will have victory over the mark of the beast.

And I saw as it were a sea of glass mingled with fire: and them that had gotten the VICTORY OVER THE BEAST, and over his image, AND OVER HIS MARK, and over the number of his name, stand on the sea of glass, having the harps of God.

Revelation 15:2

The Secret of Spiritual Teamwork

And I stood upon the sand of the sea, and saw a beast rise up out of the sea, having seven heads and ten horns, and upon his horns ten crowns, and upon his heads the name of blasphemy. And the beast which I saw was like unto a leopard, and his feet were as the feet of a bear, and his mouth as the mouth of a lion: and THE DRAGON GAVE HIM HIS POWER, AND HIS SEAT, AND GREAT AUTHORITY.

And I saw one of his heads as it were wounded to death; and his deadly wound was healed: and all the world wondered after the beast. AND THEY WORSHIPPED THE DRAGON WHICH GAVE POWER UNTO THE BEAST: and they worshipped the beast, saying, who is like unto the beast? Who is able to make war with him?...

And I beheld another beast coming up out of the earth; and he had two horns like a lamb, and he spake as a dragon. And he exerciseth all the power of the first beast before him, and CAUSETH THE EARTH AND THEM WHICH DWELL THEREIN TO WORSHIP THE FIRST BEAST, whose deadly wound was healed.

Revelation 13:1-4, 11-12

Thehe spiritual teamwork skills of the beast, the dragon and the second beast are notable and worthy of comment. Both the dragon and the second beast propped up the beast.

Wise assistants prop up their leaders to attain ultimate victory.

The dragon and the second beast were like two good assistants who magnified the powers and the strengths of their leader. Instead of each of them trying to be great, they all agreed to give their power to the beast. They established his seat and his great authority.

The dragon was a good assistant to the beast. The dragon empowered the beast. Through the activities of the dragon, the beast became more powerful and exerted more authority. To be a good assistant is to give your power to your leader. To be a good assistant is to make the seat and the authority of your leader even more secure. To be a good assistant is to empower your leader.

Whenever people are wise enough to make one person the main leader and support him in his headship, they become a formidable force. The beast, the second beast and the dragon became an amazing team that challenged Christ the Saviour and the armies of Heaven. Of course, they were no match for the Lord of Lords and the King of Kings.

And I saw the beast, and the kings of the earth, and their armies, gathered together to make war against him that sat on the horse, and against his army. And the beast was taken, and with him the false prophet that wrought miracles before him, with which he deceived them that had received the mark of the beast, and them that worshipped his image. These both were cast alive into a lake of fire burning with brimstone.

Revelation 19:19-20

Today, many people do not have the teamwork that gives power to the right person to enable him to accomplish great things. The assistants and other members of the team fight their leader instead of helping him. Because they lack this skill of lifting up the main leader, they never become the mighty force that they could be.

It is amazing that the beast, the dragon and the second beast had enough sense to form a good team to help each other to achieve their wicked goals. Many pastors do not know how to work as a team. They do not have the skills, the wisdom and the technique that the dragon, the beast and the second beast had. I have watched young missionaries fight each other about who is in charge. In charge of what? There is no point of being in charge of nothing. Why do you not help each other so that both of you become great?

When a team works well, and is successful, they all receive the same great rewards. Whenever a team wins a match, it is the whole team that receives the bonus. Equally, when the team is poor at their teamwork, they all receive the same judgment. The assistant's role is so important that his judgment is equal to the judgment of his leader.

Notice that the false prophet, the beast and the dragon were all thrown into the lake of fire. They all had the same kind of judgment because they helped each other to accomplish whatever they did. When you are a good assistant, you will share in the rewards. Every assistant will share in the judgments that come to the team. Notice how the beast and the false prophet are thrown into the same lake of fire at the same time. They are both tormented because the team is always rewarded together or judged together.

And THE DEVIL that deceived them was cast into the lake of fire and brimstone, where THE BEAST and the FALSE PROPHET are, and shall be tormented day and night forever and ever.

Revelation 20:10

VICTORY SECRET NO.12

The Secret of Defilement by Women

And I looked, and, lo, a Lamb stood on the mount Sion, and with him an hundred forty and four thousand, having his Father's name written in their foreheads.

And I heard a voice from heaven, as the voice of many waters, and as the voice of a great thunder: and I heard the voice of harpers harping with their harps: and they sung as it were a new song before the throne, and before the four beasts, and the elders: and no man could learn that song but the hundred and forty and four thousand, which were redeemed from the earth.

THESE ARE THEY WHICH WERE NOT DEFILED WITH WOMEN; FOR THEY ARE VIRGINS. THESE ARE THEY WHICH FOLLOW THE LAMB whithersoever he goeth. These were redeemed from among men, being the firstfruits unto God and to the Lamb.

And in their mouth was found no guile: for they are without fault before the throne of God.

Revelation 14:1-5

The book of Revelation clearly reveals and unveils things that are hidden from open view. Things that are not public knowledge are made known to us if we care to accept them.

Revelation means to unveil and to show something that is hidden.

We learn from the passage above that you can be defiled by women.

In the book of Revelation, one hundred and forty four thousand special people are welcomed into Heaven and the reason for their specialness is revealed in Revelation 14:4. There are three statements which reveal why they are so special.

1. **They are not defiled by women!**

2. **They are virgins!**

3. **They follow the Lamb everywhere!**

Does this mean that all those who are married and are no more virgins are defiled?

Does this mean that all those who are married and are no more virgins are unable to qualify for this holy and high status?

Have we all made the great mistake of defilement by getting married?

Has losing our virginity even in the context of marriage made us defiled Christians?

Indeed no! Being married and losing your virginity in marriage is not defilement. The Bible says clearly that it is not defilement. Marriage is actually honourable.

Marriage is honourable in all, and the bed undefiled: but whoremongers and adulterers God will judge.

Hebrews 13:4

So how does the absence of virginity defile us? Defilement is a spiritual state. To be defiled with women is to be affected spiritually by women. To be defiled by a woman is to be affected by a woman in such a way that you are not as pure and as acceptable to God as you used to be.

Obviously this is not a physical defilement of being contaminated with the bodily fluids of a woman. It is a spiritual pollution and contamination that comes from relating very intimately with women.

How does this happen? How can a woman affect you spiritually? Does this only happen when you relate intimately with a woman you are not married to?

This pollution of women can happen to anyone who is interacting with women. It happens when you lose your virginity. To lose your virginity is to have a deep, penetrating, invading, life-changing relationship with a woman in such a way that you cannot follow the Lamb everywhere.

This applies to people whether they are married or not. Your spiritual call and walk with God must not be affected by women. When this is the case, you are contaminated; and when you are contaminated you cannot follow the Lamb everywhere He goes!

You and your ministry can be contaminated by a woman you are not married to, so that you are unable to follow the Lamb everywhere. This happens when you sin with women you are not married to by committing fornication with them!

You and your ministry can also be contaminated by a woman you are married to and make you unable to follow the Lamb everywhere. This happens when you are connected to your wife in such a way that you are unwilling to sacrifice that intimacy for the will of God.

The contamination starts when there is a very deep and intimate relationship that makes you lose your spiritual identity and spiritual aloneness! Thereafter you cannot follow the Lamb everywhere.

Remember that these virgins are able to follow the Lamb everywhere. When you are too deeply connected to women (be it your wife or not your wife), you may not be able to follow the Lamb everywhere. Because you cannot follow the Lamb everywhere, you are defiled, affected or polluted, depending on what you want to call it.

Today many married ministers cannot follow the Lamb everywhere because they are too intimately connected to their wives. Many ministers are emasculated and incapable of leadership and true ministry because they are controlled by their marriages. This is probably why Jesus did not marry!

There is no way Jesus could have fulfilled the wishes of His Father in a marriage situation. His wife would not have allowed Him to go to the cross. Which woman would allow her loving "A1" husband to leave her at the tender age of thirty-three?

Even the intimate connection that Jesus had with Peter started to be a hindrance to his mission to the cross. Peter did not want Jesus to die on the cross. Peter opposed Jesus' dying on the cross for mankind.

Truly, many cannot obey God and follow the Lamb because of their deep relationships with women. Some men commit fornication and adultery and are tied down by their sins. The contamination of sexual sin and its attendant complications make it difficult to even preach the right message anymore.

I have seen many ministers destroyed and rendered incapable of following the Lamb by their intimate relationships with their wives. In the name of having a good marriage, they are no longer able to follow the Lamb everywhere.

Remember that when Eve destroyed the life of Adam, she was a wife to him. Adam was not destroyed by his secretary or his girlfriend! Eve was not a girlfriend or a strange woman when she destroyed Adam and his ministry! The inability of Adam to follow God's instruction can be directly attributed to his insistence on being close to his wife and following her into her error. Be careful of being too close to your wife and too committed to her to the extent that it takes you away from following the Lamb. No one should ever become more important than the Lamb.

When John Wesley got married he said, "I see no reason why a person should travel less or preach less in a married or unmarried state." John Wesley was less intimately connected to his wife because she was an accuser and a challenger to him. His brother on the other hand had a good intimate marriage. Amazingly, Charles Wesley, who had a good intimate marriage, completely stopped his itinerant preaching ministry so he could stay home with his loving wife.

John Wesley on the other hand, had a wicked woman as his wife so it was easier for him not to be obedient to his wife.

Many ministers of the gospel are obedient to their wives rather than being obedient to God! Amazing but true! Many ministers of the gospel are afraid to have a conflict with their wives concerning the work of God. They want peace with the woman rather than peace with God. Indeed they are truly contaminated and defiled in their service to God.

They say, "God first, family second and ministry third." This statement sounds very wise but is not found in the Bible. The first commandment is to love God. The second commandment is to love your neighbour (not your wife). Your neighbour lives in the next house and not in your house.

This is why the church is in the state it is. This is why the church has so few missionaries today! Many wives would not want to live under certain difficult conditions. They may not want to suffer. They may want a good life. This is why other religions with self-sacrificial people, who don't mind dying and never seeing their families again, are taking over entire nations whilst Christianity is declining terribly!

Generally speaking, if you tie yourself to your woman's ideas and limited vision, your ministry will never be fulfilled! Many wives are limited in their vision. You can see this short-sighted vision in most brides. Their entire focus is on the wedding, the wedding reception and the celebration of the event. Many of the young girls getting married have not thought beyond the three-hour joyous wedding experience.

Do not let your ministry be limited by the limited vision of a woman. Do not be defiled by a woman. Follow the Lamb everywhere! If you are not prepared to stand your ground against your own wife over the will of God, you will lose your importance to God.

Many times good Christian ministers of the gospel love their wives way above the required limits, creating a real alternative to God Himself. We do not read of any crowns for having a wonderful marriage. A good marriage is very important but not more important than God! A good marriage is very important but not more important than obeying the will of God!

"Thou shalt love the Lord thy God. There shall be no others before me". This is what God says. It is possible to love your wife, your family and your children way above the will of God!

Be careful that you are never contaminated and polluted by women in your service to God. Beware of defilement from the woman you are married to and also beware of defilement from the women you are not married to! Follow the Lamb everywhere! Do not be defiled by women!

VICTORY SECRET NO. 13

The Secret of Spiritual Power

AND I SAW THREE UNCLEAN SPIRITS LIKE FROGS COME OUT OF THE MOUTH OF THE DRAGON, AND OUT OF THE MOUTH OF THE BEAST, AND OUT OF THE MOUTH OF THE FALSE PROPHET.

For they are THE SPIRITS OF DEVILS, WORKING MIRACLES, which go forth unto the kings of the earth and of the whole world, TO GATHER THEM to the battle of that great day of God Almighty.

Revelation 16:13-14

O nce again, we see a great revelation about how spiritual power works. The dragon, the beast and the false prophet formed an amazing team and exerted immense spiritual power in the world. Even though they were defeated, their manoeuvres, actions and operations reveal a lot about how spiritual power works.

1. Spiritual power works through unity.

And I saw three unclean spirits like frogs come out of the mouth of the dragon, and out of the mouth of the beast, and out of the mouth of the false prophet.

Revelation 16:13

The dragon, the beast and the false prophet were united in speaking the same things. Out of their mouths came spirits that looked like frogs. The dragon had a frog coming out of his mouth! The beast had a frog coming out of his mouth! The false prophet also had a frog coming out of his mouth. They were saying the same things and producing identical spirits that were working together. So instead of one frog, there were three spiritual frogs that were working out the evils in the world.

Today, Christians cannot see the powerlessness that they live in because they are not united and not joined in what they are doing. Unity is the ultimate multiplier of the anointing. Unity is a profound multiplier of the power in a mantle. If you can be united with another, you will increase greatly. Many ministers stand alone without help, without unity and without loyalty. Satan knows the power of unity and used it when it mattered. Because satan knows the power of unity, he constantly causes disunity, accusation and the breakdown of the family spirit.

If you cannot learn from all the other teachings about unity and loyalty, perhaps you may want to now learn from the unity displayed by the dragon, the beast and the false prophet.

2. Spiritual power to perform miracles is released through the mouth.

...they are the spirits of devils, working miracles ...

Revelation 16:14

Through the spirits that were coming out of the mouths of the dragon, the beast and the false prophet, many important things were taking place. Spiritual power to perform miracles was released as they opened their mouths and spiritual frogs came out. The exact mechanism for the working of miracles is revealed in this amazing revelation. As they spoke, frog spirits came out of their mouth and performed the miracles. The power of the spoken word is taught all through the scriptures. God opened His mouth and said, "Let there be light." The power to create the whole world was released by these words. Jesus said, "The words I speak to you are Spirit and life." Once again, if you do not want to learn the secret of spiritual power from God the Father or Jesus, perhaps you can learn it now from the operations of the false prophet, the beast and the dragon.

The beast, the false prophet and the dragon know the power of the spoken word. They know the secret of spiritual power. That is why they try to keep people away from the words of God's anointed prophets. That is why devils inspire people to say negative things about themselves and about others. Many words that are spoken are spiritual creatures coming out of people's mouths, performing amazing things in the physical realm. Watch out for your mouth. Watch out for the words that you hear! Watch out for things that are spoken! Many of them are living spirits.

In ministering to the sick, it is important to call out miracles and declare healings. The secret of spiritual power is to speak the Word and the mighty Holy Spirit will perform exactly what you are speaking. Do not only say what God has done. Declare what He is doing. Perform miracles with your mouth. Declare the blessings over the people and they will happen! Declare protection over the people, and it will happen! Declare healing over the people and it will come to pass!

3.   Spiritual power to gather crowds is released through the mouth.

They are the spirits of devils, working miracles, which go forth unto the kings of the earth and of the whole world, TO GATHER THEM...

Revelation 16:14

The three frogs are the three spirits that go out of the mouth of these three characters. The beast, the false prophet and the dragon release these spirits through their mouths. The spirits accomplished two things. The spirits performed miracles and also gathered the whole world together for a battle. Once again, we see the dragon, the false prophet and the beast using spiritual power to gather crowds together.

Jesus said, "The words that I speak, they are Spirit and life." Many people also gathered to hear Jesus speak. Great multitudes came to *hear* Jesus and to be healed. They did not just come to be healed, they came to *hear first* and be healed also. His words were so powerful and His miracles, so amazing. Through this great combination, thousands of people gathered to hear Jesus speak. Jesus gathered crowds and ministered to them through His powerful preaching and teaching ministry.

But so much the more went there a fame abroad of him: and GREAT MULTITUDES CAME TOGETHER TO HEAR, and to be healed by him of their infirmities.

Luke 5:15

The devil, in seeking to mimic the ministry of Jesus, uses the same strategy to gather crowds. Spiritual forces to gather crowds and influence them to kill each other are released through the mouth. Perhaps, you have not understood the importance of learning how to preach powerfully and beautifully. It is a secret you must learn from Jesus.

Perhaps, you have failed to learn the secret of spiritual power from Jesus Himself.

Today, you can see how the enemies of Christ have used the very same principles of spiritual power to advance the cause of evil. Today, satan uses the power of television and radio to gather people for evil activities. There are evil spirits coming out of the television, radio and the Internet all the time, gathering people to many evil meetings.

It is time to rise and speak words through the pulpit, the radio and the Internet and gather people to the assembly of the saints. It is time to gather large crowds through the words from your mouth on radio, and television. God is showing you the secrets of the spiritual power that is used to gather crowds.

The Secret of the Position of your Candlestick

And I turned to see the voice that spake with me. And being turned, I saw seven golden candlesticks; AND IN THE MIDST OF THE SEVEN CANDLESTICKS ONE LIKE UNTO THE SON OF MAN . . .

The mystery of the seven stars which thou sawest in my right hand, and the seven golden candlesticks. The seven stars are the angels of the seven churches: and the seven candlesticks which thou sawest are the seven churches.

Revelation 1:12-13, 20

Remember therefore from whence thou art fallen, and repent, and do the first works; or else I will come unto thee quickly, and WILL REMOVE THY CANDLESTICK OUT OF HIS PLACE, except thou repent.

Revelation 2:5

The secret of the position of the candlestick is the greatest secret of prosperity. It is a secret that is not taught in schools, seminars and universities. It is the secret of where you are positioned relative to Jesus Christ. It is the secret of where you are positioned relative to the all-important river of life running near to you.

WHERE YOU ARE POSITIONED IS MORE IMPORTANT THAN WHAT YOU DO! Your closeness to God is more important than the things you do. The only punishment Jesus offered to the disobedient church was to change their position relative to Himself. Mercy! The question of being close to or far from the Lord changes everything for you. CLOSENESS IS THE KEY TO PROSPERITY AND FLOURISHING.

For a minister, being close to God is more important than anything else. Spending time with God is the most important activity you can engage in. *It is the position of the candlestick that matters. Jesus stands in the midst of the candlesticks.* The hours of prayer and the hours of waiting in His presence make up the most important activity of your life!

Every country is blessed with a number of rivers. Your best bet is to locate yourself by a river and stay close to it. Rivers are not found everywhere. That is why most great civilizations are built around rivers. For instance Egypt was built around the River Nile. London was built around the River Thames. Paris was built around the River Seine. Seoul was built around the River Han. New York is near the Hudson River. Chicago is on Lake Michigan. Moscow is on the Moskva River. Dubai is on the Persian Gulf. Vienna is near the Danube River. Rome was built near the Tiber River. Tokyo was built around the River Sumida. Sao Paulo was built around the River Tiete. Melbourne is built around the River Yarra. Montreal is built around the River St. Lawrence. Madrid is built around the River Manzanares. Kiev is built around the River Dnieper. Lisbon is built around the River Tagus.

Anointing and even prosperity are like rivers given to bless the nations. Position yourself near to what God has divinely provided. For example, many people who live in Seattle, where Bill Gates lives, are millionaires! Your secret to prosperity is not in your cleverness, your education or your hard work. Your secret to the anointing is not in your cleverness, your education or your hard work. Your secret to prosperity is being close to certain people.

Your greatest secret is to recognize *where* God is working and associate yourself closely with that river! Flourish now by your closeness to the rivers and prophetic determinations of the Lord. You are a tree of righteousness and you must be planted next to a river.

The Key of Closeness is the Key of Prosperity

1. **The Lord Jesus is standing in the midst of the candlesticks: stay close to the Lord and prosper.**

    The mystery of the seven stars which thou sawest in my right hand, and the seven golden candlesticks. The seven stars are the angels of the seven churches: and the seven candlesticks which thou sawest are the seven churches.

    Revelation 1:20

    You and I are the candlesticks. Our position relative to Jesus is all that matters.

    The presence of Jesus in the midst of us is all we need. Watch out for the presence of Jesus in the midst of the candlestick. That is the thing to look out for. Jesus threatens to remove your candlestick from its position as your punishment for not loving Him with first love.

2.   **You are part of a spiritual tree: stay connected and prosper.**

Abide in me, and I in you. As the branch cannot bear fruit of itself, except it abide in the vine; no more can ye, except ye abide in me.

I am the vine, YE ARE THE BRANCHES: He that ABIDETH IN ME, and I in him, the same bringeth forth much fruit: for without me ye can do nothing.

IF A MAN ABIDE NOT in me, he is cast forth as a branch, and IS WITHERED; and men gather them, and cast them into the fire, and they are burned.

John 15: 4-6

Your key to flourishing as a branch is to stay connected to your spiritual tree. Abide in that very close position of being attached to the vine. Do not be separated in any way. Disconnection and detachment are the master keys to your withering. Watch your connection to the tree! It is your close attachment that leads to life. Jesus says, abide in me! Stay close to me!

3.   **Jesus is the vine and the apostles and prophets are primary and secondary branches of the vine: stay close to your apostles and prosper.**

Abide in me, and I in you. As the branch cannot bear fruit of itself, except it abide in the vine; no more can ye, except ye abide in me.

I am the vine, YE ARE THE BRANCHES: He that abideth in me, and I in him, the same bringeth forth much fruit: for without me ye can do nothing.

If a man abide not in me, he is cast forth as a branch, and is withered; and men gather them, and cast them into the fire, and they are burned.

John 15: 4-6

The apostles are primary branches. The prophets are the secondary branches of that tree. The pastors, evangelists and teachers are the tertiary branches of the tree. Ordinary church members are also connected to the tree. Your survival is connected to your ability to maintain the closest connection to the apostles and prophets God has given you.

4.   God will give you pastors after His heart: stay close to your pastor and flourish.

And I WILL GIVE YOU PASTORS ACCORDING TO MINE HEART, which shall feed you with knowledge and understanding.

And it shall come to pass, when ye be multiplied and increased in the land, in those days, saith the Lord, they shall say no more, The ark of the covenant of the Lord: neither shall it come to mind: neither shall they remember it; neither shall they visit it; neither shall that be done any more.

Jeremiah 3:15-16

God chooses pastors for you. God gives pastors to us. God sends men of God into our lives. You don't choose your teachers or fathers. God chooses them for you. If we had the choice to be born in Africa or Germany most of us would choose to be born in Germany. But God chose your country for you. God also chose a pastor for you. God will increase and multiply you as you stay close to Him.

5.   You are a tree, the planting of the Lord: stay close to the water and flourish.

To appoint unto them that mourn in Zion, to give unto them beauty for ashes, the oil of joy for mourning, the garment of praise for the spirit of heaviness; that they might be called trees of righteousness, THE PLANTING OF THE LORD, that he might be glorified.

Isaiah 61:3

The future of a tree is dependent on its closeness to water. That is why the positioning of the tree in relation to the river is the greatest secret of prosperity for the tree. Refugees are always in great difficulty because they are displaced from their rightful places. Do not become a spiritual refugee.

And he shall be like a tree planted by the rivers of water, that bringeth forth his fruit in his season; his leaf also shall not wither; and whatsoever he doeth shall prosper.

Psalm 1:3

6.   **It is the grafting of the wild branches to the tree that gives it life: stay close and prosper.**

And if some of the branches be broken off, and thou, being a wild olive tree, wert grafted in among them, and with them partakest of the root and fatness of the olive tree;

Romans 11:17

The grafted branch partakes of the root and fatness of the olive tree. This is the great key to prosperity. Being close enough and being grafted to your spiritual tree will begin to connect you to the roots, depths and oily fatness of the olive tree. Your connection to the men God has chosen for you is your master key to the oil and the fatness.

7.   **The closest to the shepherd is the safest.**

And there were in the same country shepherds abiding in the field, keeping watch over their flock by night.

Luke 2:8

While shepherds watched their flocks by night! Shepherds were abiding in the field and watching over the flocks by night. The shepherds were watching over their flocks in the night, in the time of their greatest danger. If you are a sheep, then your safest spot is to lie closely to the shepherd. When the bear and the lion attacked the sheep, David, the shepherd, rose up and saved the lives of the helpless sheep.

And David said unto Saul, Thy servant kept his father's sheep, and there came a lion, and a bear, and took a lamb out of the flock: And I went out after him, and smote him, and delivered it out of his mouth: and when he arose against me, I caught him by his beard, and smote him, and slew him.

1 Samuel 17: 34-35

That is the great blessing of being close to the Lord who is the greatest shepherd. Your good shepherd is going to run after the bear and lion of your life and save you. Be close to your shepherd and prosper!

Every step I take that makes me closer to God, is the best step I could ever make as a minister.

Every activity, which makes me seek the Lord, to find His Presence and to be with Him, is the right thing to do!

I want my candlestick to be the nearest to Jesus. Don't you want your candlestick to be near Jesus? Your flourishing and your prosperity depend on you being close to Jesus!

VICTORY SECRET NO. 15

The Secret of Spiritual Hatred

Unto the angel of the church of Ephesus write; These things saith he that holdeth the seven stars in his right hand, who walketh in the midst of the seven golden candlesticks; I know thy works, and thy labour, and thy patience, and how thou canst not bear them which are evil: and thou hast tried them which say they are apostles, and are not, and hast found them liars: And hast borne, and hast patience, and for my name's sake hast laboured, and hast not fainted.

Nevertheless I have somewhat against thee, because thou hast left thy first love. Remember therefore from whence thou art fallen, and repent, and do the first works; or else I will come unto thee quickly, and will remove thy candlestick out of his place, except thou repent. BUT THIS THOU HAST, THAT THOU HATEST THE DEEDS OF THE NICOLAITANS, WHICH I ALSO HATE.

Revelation 2:1-6

Hatred is the strongest negative passion a person can have. Hatred is different from a dislike or distaste. Amazingly, the Ephesian church was recommended for their spiritual hatred.

What is hatred? It is an intense and passionate dislike for something that makes you want to eliminate it from your life.

WHOSOEVER HATETH HIS BROTHER IS A MURDERER: and ye know that no murderer hath eternal life abiding in him.

1 John 3:15

He that hates his brother wipes out his brother from the surface of this earth forever. All through the Bible you see the importance of wiping out things absolutely and completely. Having spiritual hatred is an important spiritual achievement. Many ministers do not have enough spiritual hatred for certain things, as they should. You will one day have to prove whether you have enough spiritual hatred or not. You will one day have to prove whether you have the spiritual guts to wipe out certain things completely.

Saul the king did not have enough spiritual hatred to wipe out Agag the king and all the Amalekites. This cost him his ministry, his position with God and his life.

And the Lord sent thee on a journey, and said, Go and utterly destroy the sinners the Amalekites, and fight against them until they be consumed. Wherefore then didst thou not obey the voice of the Lord, but didst fly upon the spoil, and didst evil in the sight of the Lord?

1 Samuel 15:18-19

The Israelites did not have the spiritual hatred to wipe out the Philistines and other tribes they met in the Promised Land. Only Judah and Simeon were bold enough to fight with the Philistines and wipe them out.

And Judah went with Simeon his brother, and they slew the Canaanites that inhabited Zephath, and utterly destroyed it. And the name of the city was called Hormah.

Judges 1:17

The rest of the tribes of Israel simply did not have enough spiritual hatred to wipe out the other tribes. And it was these very tribes who rose up to fight Israel in the coming years.

Neither did Manasseh drive out the inhabitants of Bethshean and her towns, nor Taanach and her towns, nor the inhabitants of Dor and her towns, nor the inhabitants of Ibleam and her towns, nor the inhabitants of Megiddo and her towns: but the Canaanites would dwell in that land.

And it came to pass, when Israel was strong, that they put the Canaanites to tribute, and did not utterly drive them out.

Neither did Ephraim drive out the Canaanites that dwelt in Gezer; but the Canaanites dwelt in Gezer among them.

Neither did Zebulun drive out the inhabitants of Kitron, nor the inhabitants of Nahalol; but the Canaanites dwelt among them, and became tributaries.

Neither did Asher drive out the inhabitants of Accho, nor the inhabitants of Zidon, nor of Ahlab, nor of Achzib, nor of Helbah, nor of Aphik, nor of Rehob: But the Asherites dwelt among the Canaanites, the inhabitants of the land: for they did not drive them out.

Neither did Naphtali drive out the inhabitants of Bethshemesh, nor the inhabitants of Bethanath; but he dwelt among the Canaanites, the inhabitants of the land: nevertheless the inhabitants of Bethshemesh and of Bethanath became tributaries unto them.

Judges 1:27-33

What is there in your life that God teaches you to hate and to wipe out? There are many things you have to learn to hate. Strife and disloyalty in all their forms must be hated by wise ministers. People who toy with dangerous things, often get bitten by them. You may have heard about the famous snake handler who died handling one of his snakes. Most people just kill snakes when they find them. Just hate all dangerous things and wipe them out! There is no point in playing with your life.

I have watched as people have toyed with disloyalty. I once visited a church and preached strongly against disloyalty. The pastor was very blessed and realized that his church and ministry were being destroyed by those who were treacherous, disloyal and accusative. He immediately launched a permanent crusade against these elements in his church.

On the other hand, I also visited another church outside Ghana and preached exactly the same message against destabilizing pastors and disloyal elements. The pastor was appreciative of the stabilizing message and even commended me for it. He said my message was needed in the body of Christ. However, he did not develop a hatred for these things, as he could have. Indeed, a disloyal member of the church came up to him after my message and complained about my preaching on disloyalty. To my amazement, he told the treacherous church member, "Do not let the preaching on disloyalty affect you too much."

Then he praised the treacherous fellow and told him, "You have done well to endure the teaching on disloyalty that is directed against you."

This pastor tolerated treacherous elements in the church and even promoted them. I noticed one day that he had actually elevated them to the highest possible rank in his church.

Obviously this pastor did not understand the need to hate and wipe disloyalty from his ministry. Remember that God commended the church by saying, "I know you hate these things..."

Jesus hated disloyalty above all the sins and wickedness He met on earth. He told his disciples "It would have been better if Judas had not been born."

... It had been good for that man if he had not been born.

Matthew 26:24

Notice that Jesus did not say it would have been better if Pontius Pilate, the Roman soldiers, Zacchaeus, the woman caught in adultery or even the woman of Samaria had not been born. Jesus' attitude towards the disloyalty of Judas was far more negative than His attitude towards anything else. It is often better if a disloyal person is not born! Learn to hate the things that Jesus hates. Learn to love the things that Jesus loves.

VICTORY SECRET NO.16

The Secret of
Survival Abilities

He that hath an ear, let him hear what the Spirit saith
unto the churches; To him that overcometh will I give
to eat of the tree of life, which is in the midst of the
paradise of God.

And unto the angel of the church in Smyrna write;
These things saith the first and the last, which was
dead, and is alive; I know thy works, and tribulation,
and poverty, (but thou art rich) and I know the
blasphemy of them which say they are Jews, and are
not, but are the synagogue of Satan. Fear none of those
things which thou shalt suffer: behold, the devil shall
cast some of you into prison, that ye may be tried; and
ye shall have tribulation ten days: be thou faithful unto
death, and I will give thee a crown of life.

He that hath an ear, let him hear what the Spirit saith
unto the churches; He that overcometh shall not be
hurt of the second death.

Revelation 2:7-11

Every minister should be aware that there are two spiritual markers in their lives that can be seen from Heaven above and are being monitored all the time. The first thing that is seen is YOUR WORKS. The second thing that is seen is YOUR ABILITY TO SURVIVE.

To survive is to be able to go through something difficult, to remain in existence, to get along, to be unaffected and happy, in spite of circumstances and occurrences around you.

Most people are aware of the fact that their works are being monitored. Most of us are conscious of the fact that when we get to Heaven our works will follow us and we will be judged for how much work we have done. We will also be judged by the quality of our works.

However, there is another thing about you that is being monitored. This reality is not so apparent and also not so easy to understand. *God is observing the things you are surviving and the things you are going through.* The works you have accomplished, as well as the things you are going through are the two markers that are under observation from above.

I once read something that Derek Prince had written. I did not understand it when I read it. He said he was watching television and saw a young minister speaking. This young minister was describing the things that he had accomplished and how God was using him to do many great works. Then, he made a very important comment. He said, a time would come when this young minister would learn that it is not what he had accomplished that mattered, but what he had been able to go through that would matter. In other words, the ability of this man of God to survive difficulty and hardships would become important and not his accomplishments.

All through the letters to the seven churches, the angel commends the church for its survival of negative and difficult things. God is looking out for our works but He is also looking out for our ability to survive difficult things.

"I know your works and your tribulation and your poverty" (Revelation 2:9). In other words, God is marking your accomplishments but He is also marking your tribulation and poverty. The word "survive" means to be able to go through something difficult, to remain in existence, to overcome adversity, to be unaffected and happy, in spite of circumstances and occurrences around you.

It is what you have survived and what you have gone through, without being destroyed, that makes you a spiritual giant. When Jesus wanted to identify Himself, He identified Himself by His wounds and scars and not by the souls that He had won.

When Jesus is spoken of in the book of Revelation, He is spoken of as the Lamb that was slain. The experience of becoming a lamb and allowing Himself to be slain seems to be of far greater importance than the people He healed whilst He was on earth.

Let us now take a look at how the ability to survive negative and difficult things is noted by the angel of each church in the book of Revelation.

1. **You will be marked for your works and FOR YOUR ABILITY TO SURVIVE DELAYS.**

    I know thy works, and thy labour, and THY PATIENCE, and how thou canst not bear them which are evil: and thou hast tried them which say they are apostles, and are not, and hast found them liars: And HAST BORNE, AND HAST PATIENCE, and for my name's sake hast laboured, and hast not fainted.

    Revelation 2:2-3

The church in Ephesus was marked for its works and its ability to survive delays. That is why God complimented them on their patience. You are being assessed in Heaven on your patience and your ability to bear delays.

2. **You will be marked for your works and FOR YOUR SURVIVAL OF TRIBULATION, POVERTY and BLASPHEMY.**

I know thy works, and TRIBULATION, and POVERTY, (but thou art rich) and I know the BLASPHEMY of them which say they are Jews, and are not, but are the synagogue of Satan.

Revelation 2:9

Tribulation is severe persecution and intense trouble. Few people are able to make it through times of trouble. Your ability to survive intense accusations, trials and troubles will make you stand out in Heaven. Blasphemy is vilification, slander and injurious speech spoken against another's good name. Many ministers endure injurious and reproachful words spoken by detractors who despise God's servants.

It is not that easy to persist onwards in the midst of bad and negative stories, jokes and mockery about yourself. It is not easy to hear yourself being misrepresented and taken out of context by mocking birds and accusative voices that hate God's servants.

One of the amazing realities is that ministers of the gospel are ready to jump on the bandwagon and criticize their own fellow ministers. Actually ministers of God may be their own worst accusers.

Many ministers of the gospel are waiting to hear something negative about their fellow ministers. Remember that Jesus Christ was crucified by fellow religious men, called Pharisees and Sadducees, who wanted to see the end of this inspiring young preacher who made them look so dull and uninspiring.

Jesus Christ's ministry brought out the hypocrisy of the established clergy. They hated him because people flocked to see and to hear reality. The pastors of that day were so happy to see Jesus crucified. Jesus survived extreme hatred! Even on the cross, He forgave the slandering, lying and mocking human beings who gathered around to destroy Him.

At a certain stage in the ministry, it is not what you have accomplished that matters. It is what you have survived that matters! Your ability to survive poverty is a great accomplishment in ministry.

If God gives you poverty and you are able to survive it, that is a great accomplishment in ministry! If you are able to survive extreme slander, backbiting and blasphemy, that is also an achievement and is well noted in Heaven.

If you are married to an accuser who casts upon you the most preposterous suggestions of evil-doing, and are still able to persist in ministry, that is an achievement well-noted in Heaven. Most people who are married to accusative people limit their ministry to the areas that the accuser and controller of their lives find acceptable. They do this to preserve their marriages. Few people, like John Wesley, are able to persist to a high level of fruitfulness in the midst of incredible allegations, slander and accusations.

3.   **You will be marked for your works *and* FOR YOUR ABILITY TO SURVIVE WHERE SATAN DWELLS.**

I know thy works, and where thou dwellest, even WHERE SATAN'S SEAT is: and thou holdest fast my name, and hast not denied my faith, even in those days wherein Antipas was my faithful martyr, who was slain among you, WHERE SATAN DWELLETH.

Revelation 2:13

Ministering where satan dwells is a well-noted achievement. There are pastors who are ashamed of their small churches because they compare themselves with the wrong things. You cannot compare a ministry where satan dwells with a ministry where satan only visits.

Where satan dwells is where he is strong, established and in control. Everyone is strong and established in his own house. In the world today, there are areas where churches are not even allowed to exist. Satan's presence is marked by the absolute rejection of the church. Satan's presence is also noted in places where they do not even believe in the existence of God. Such places are very difficult to minister in and the churches there are very small.

I once ministered in a place that had about two hundred and fifty million people. There were only one hundred and fifty pastors left in that region. Most of the pastors in that region of the world had fled. The few remaining churches were small and were not even allowed to meet on Sundays. There are countries without a single church. There are indeed places where satan dwells, making it impossible for the church to survive. It is important to have pastors and ministers in such places. We are the light of the world. If there is no pastor and no church, it means that that area is in total darkness.

4. **You will be marked for your works *and* FOR SURVIVING DOUBTS, BITTERNESS AND DELAYS.**

   And unto the angel of the church in Thyatira write; These things saith the Son of God, who hath his eyes like unto a flame of fire, and his feet are like fine brass; I know thy works, and charity, and service, and FAITH, AND THY PATIENCE, and thy works; and the last to be more than the first.

   Revelation 2:18-19

   Your ability to maintain faith and patience is well noted in Heaven. There are many things that throw up questions into our hearts. Why did God not answer this prayer? Why did this fail? I once felt that God had spoken to me. I felt sure that I had His direction for my life. After a while, I realized that I had made a mistake and gone astray.

This brought up questions about other things I had felt that God had spoken to me about. It is not easy to set aside doubts when you have made one terrible mistake. How can you be sure you are being led by the Holy Spirit? How can you be sure God is the one speaking now? To survive things that stir up doubts in your heart is a great achievement. Many people stop believing in the supernatural things of God after experiencing such strong doubts.

For instance, many pastors do not pray for the sick any more. Many ministers do not cast out devils or minister the spirit to anyone. They would rather take some medicine and send the church member to the hospital. Supernatural things are vague, distant and doubtful to many ministers of the gospel. Many of us have lost the faith and are not able to believe much after experiencing doubt-creating events. This is why Paul said at the end of his ministry, "I have kept the faith." It is indeed a great achievement to keep the faith.

Sometimes, people's response to your great love and efforts is so appalling. You even wonder whether it is worth being in the ministry. I remember a pastor who received a special offering on his fortieth birthday. The offering from the congregation was so small that it ministered very negative feelings to the man of God. He no longer felt it was worth being a pastor to those ungrateful people. Indeed, doubts about his calling began looming in his heart.

I remember another pastor who started branches of his church. All the pastors he sent out to begin these churches turned against him and betrayed him. From that time, he was filled with doubts and questions about the need to establish churches. It is a great blessing to be able to maintain and keep your faith. The ability to keep the faith and dissolve your doubts is well noted in the heavens.

5.	**You will be marked for your works and FOR SURVIVING IN A WEAKENED STATE.**

I know thy works: behold, I have set before thee an open door, and no man can shut it: for THOU HAST A LITTLE STRENGTH, and hast kept my word, and hast not denied my name.

Revelation 3:8

When your strength is small, you have been weakened in ministry. There are many things that can weaken you in ministry. There are shocks, unexpected events, heartbreaks, disappointments, failure, the loss of loved ones, death, sickness and tragedies that can weaken your resolve to serve God.

Many people grow weaker as they get older. Experiences make them weaker. God recommends and rewards those who keep the faith even in their weakened state. This is why we must serve the Lord when we are young.

In your youthful state, there are not many things that may weaken your resolve and faith in God.

VICTORY SECRET NO.17

The Secret of "Be thou Faithful Unto Death"

And unto the angel of the church in Smyrna write; These things saith the first and the last, which was dead, and is alive; I know thy works, and tribulation, and poverty, (but thou art rich) and I know the blasphemy of them which say they are Jews, and are not, but are the synagogue of Satan. Fear none of those things which thou shalt suffer: behold, the devil shall cast some of you into prison, that ye may be tried; and ye shall have tribulation ten days: BE THOU FAITHFUL UNTO DEATH, AND I WILL GIVE THEE A CROWN OF LIFE.

He that hath an ear, let him hear what the Spirit saith unto the churches; He that overcometh shall not be hurt of the second death.

Revelation 2:8-11

Do you want to receive a crown of life in Heaven? The crown of life is given to people who have been faithful unto death. To be faithful unto death means you were loyal until you died. Death is the end of our lives on this earth. God has called us to be faithful unto death and not just for a season. Today, many people are faithful for a season. You can lift up the standard of your faithfulness and be faithful unto death. Death must be your finishing line. You must be at my funeral or I must be at yours. We must not quarrel and break our friendship before death comes. We must not turn away from our calling until death takes us away. We must be faithful unto death!

Many people are nice and good for a period but are not faithful unto death. Many people are faithful for a season. God is looking for people who will be faithful unto death. Our obedience to His will is not just for the next five years! Our faithfulness to the call is not just until you are forty years old! The faithfulness God requires is faithfulness unto death! That is the kind of faithfulness that wins the crown.

1. **"Be thou faithful unto death" applies to important relationships:**

And he that overcometh, and keepeth my works unto the end, to him will I give power over the nations:

Revelation 2:26

You must believe that the end of important relationships is death. Have relationships that will only end at the graveside where you say goodbye to each other. "I will either attend your funeral or you will attend mine" - that is what you must say about your important relationships. Your faithfulness must be unto death. Faithfulness and loyalty "till death us do part" has great rewards. You will be made to rule the nations if you can achieve this great feat of loyalty unto death.

Do not think that loyalty unto death is the same as blindness, becoming a zombie or joining a cult. People who despise faithfulness and loyalty are inexperienced in the things of God. To build any thing large and great, and to bear fruit for God, you need loyalty, commitment of the highest order and faithfulness to the end!

2.   "Be thou faithful unto death" applies to your marriage:

The wife is bound by the law AS LONG AS HER HUSBAND LIVETH; but if her husband be dead, she is at liberty to be married to whom she will; only in the Lord.

1 Corinthians 7:39

Plan to stay married to the same person till you die. Today, many people have opened the door to divorce in their lives. How do they do this? By thinking to themselves that divorce is an option. Older couples never considered divorce as an option. Modern Christians consider the changing of husbands and wives as a real possibility. Because of this, it happens much more frequently. Older marriages from the older era rarely considered the option of divorce. It was just out of the question. The understanding was that you stick with whomever you married till death parts you. This would be so even if it was a bad marriage. This mentality blocks the spirit of divorce. Remember that thoughts are spirits. The presence of certain thoughts shows the presence of certain spirits. You can block out the spirit of divorce by refusing to consider the option of changing your partner even if things are very bad.

3.   "Be thou faithful unto death" applies to your church membership:

And he shall be like a tree planted by the rivers of water, that bringeth forth his fruit in his season; his leaf also shall not wither; and whatsoever he doeth shall prosper.

Psalm 1:3

You are a tree planted by the rivers of water. Trees are usually planted in one place for their entire lives. Trees are faithful unto death. When God likens you to a tree, He is showing you the key to prosperity and stability. Church members must see the need to be faithful unto death. When you join a church, plan to be faithful unto death. In so doing, you, your children and your family will be greatly blessed through the church. People who join churches for one or two years and move on never really benefit from being in the church.

4. **"Be thou faithful unto death" applies to your relationship with your pastor:**

And Elijah said unto Elisha, Tarry here, I pray thee; for the Lord hath sent me to Bethel. And Elisha said unto him, AS THE LORD LIVETH, AND AS THY SOUL LIVETH, I WILL NOT LEAVE THEE. So they went down to Bethel.

2 Kings 2:2

Elisha's faithfulness to Elijah was unto death. This is why Elijah received a double portion of the anointing. He was faithful unto death. People who are faithful unto death deserve a greater reward. A crown of life awaits those who are faithful unto death.

There are many people who join the church and write letters to the pastor telling him how they love him and how they are blessed in the church. Do not be surprised when such people walk away unceremoniously. Talk is cheap but faithfulness is not that cheap. "…A faithful man, who can find?" (Proverbs 20:6). Indeed, who can find a church member who is faithful unto death?

Be thou faithful unto death! God wants you to be faithful to your pastor till you die.

I once met a man who had left his church and joined another. I asked, "Why are you doing that? You used to be so close to your pastor?"

He said, "I know all my pastor's sermons. There is nothing new that he can teach me. That is why I left."

Amazing! There are people who speak with such amazing arrogance. Pride and arrogance will not allow you to be faithful unto death. You must learn how to stay close for many years without becoming arrogant.

5. "Be thou faithful unto death" applies to the call of God:

For the gifts and calling of God are without repentance.

Romans 11:29

God does not change His mind about His calling on your life. If He called you when you were twenty-one years old, that call is in full operation even at sixty. There is no change as far as God is concerned. It is important that you think of your calling as something you have to do until you actually die. You are not called until you are fifty. You are called until death. There is nothing like retirement in the ministry. At every age and at every stage, there are great things you can do for the Lord.

It is a great tragedy when people shift from being preachers to being motivational speakers. They leave the wisdom of God and exchange it for human ideas. God did not call us to give clever speeches. God called us to be inspired by the Holy Spirit and moved by the Holy Spirit to speak the Word of God. Holy men of God must be moved by the Spirit to speak the Word of God. God called us to speak the wisdom that comes from above.

Do not exchange God's wisdom for human wisdom. Do not lower yourself and become a politician instead of a pastor. The call of God is without repentance! Do not lower yourself to become a businessman instead of a pastor. You must be faithful unto death in your call to be a minister.

6. **"Be thou faithful unto death" applies to the message you preach:**

As I besought thee to abide still at Ephesus, when I went into Macedonia, that thou mightest **CHARGE SOME THAT THEY TEACH NO OTHER DOCTRINE,** Neither give heed to fables and endless genealogies, which minister questions, rather than godly edifying which is in faith: so do.

Now the end of the commandment is charity out of a pure heart, and of a good conscience, and of faith unfeigned: From which some having **SWERVED HAVE TURNED ASIDE UNTO VAIN JANGLING.**

1 Timothy 1:3-6

The scripture above shows how Paul had to warn Timothy to stop people from teaching other doctrines. Today, many are swerving aside from the true gospel. Unfortunately, some great men of God are also engaged in "vain jangling". This "vain jangling" is ministered to thousands of people as the Word of God.

Today, many people cannot preach the gospel of Jesus Christ. It is all about money, prosperity or success. Success and money is not the gospel of Jesus Christ. A true minister of God must stay faithful to the original gospel. This faithfulness to the original gospel must be unto death. Our very last breath must declare that Jesus Christ died on the cross for our sins. Our last words must be about the blood of Jesus through which we are saved.

The gospel of Jesus Christ is not something meant for Sunday school and the children's church. Adults need to hear from pastors who are faithful to the gospel message. Those who are faithful unto death with the gospel message will receive the crown of life.

VICTORY SECRET NO.18

The Secret of "The Word of My Patience"

Behold, I will make them of the synagogue of Satan, which say they are Jews, and are not, but do lie; behold, I will make them to come and worship before thy feet, and to know that I have loved thee. BECAUSE THOU HAST KEPT THE WORD OF MY PATIENCE, I ALSO WILL KEEP THEE FROM THE HOUR OF TEMPTATION, which shall come upon all the world, to try them that dwell upon the earth.

Behold, I come quickly: hold that fast which thou hast, that no man take thy crown.

HIM THAT OVERCOMETH WILL I MAKE A PILLAR IN THE TEMPLE OF MY GOD, and he shall go no more out: and I will write upon him the name of my God, and the name of the city of my God, which is new Jerusalem, which cometh down out of heaven from my God: and I will write upon him my new name.

Revelation 3:9-12

T he call of God is "the word of my patience". "'The word of my patience" is a word that needs patience for its fulfilment. You can only obey God's call with great patience. Long forbearance, patient waiting and patiently working for years are what you need to successfully obey the call of God.

If you are looking for a quick fix you will have to attend to another type of work. Are you ready for a job that involves your whole life and takes a very long time to accomplish?

Keeping "the word of His patience" is the key qualification to becoming a pillar in the house of God. A pillar in the house of God is a prominent member, a key personality, a significant player and an indispensable person in the house of God.

In Heaven, your importance is guaranteed because you were able to survive life and ministry that require so much patience.

Patiently going through God's choices for you is the ultimate test on earth. John Wesley, Adoniram Judson, William Carey, James McKeon and the other great missionaries of our time passed the ultimate test with flying colours, often dying without any relief. They lived their lives and patiently obeyed the call of God. The call of God took their entire lives. Because they obeyed "the word of His patience" they will be very important in Heaven.

Who Should be a Pillar?

There is a great lesson to learn from God's choice of whom to reward. Who did God make into pillars in His house? He makes people who have kept "the word of His patience" into pillars.

Who then should you make a pillar in your church? Many people are made into pillars in churches for the wrong reasons. A pillar is someone who is elevated to become a bishop, a pastor, a leader or a prominent person in the church.

When someone has been around for a long time, it is a sign that he has patiently stayed in the church, allowing it to grow. When you appoint people who do not have many years of consistent service, you make great mistakes in the church. Electing newcomers to prominent positions in the church just because they are rich or famous is a great mistake. It's like setting up a great building on twigs and little branches. It will just be a matter time before destruction sets in. Follow the wisdom of keeping "the word of my patience". Reward faithfulness! Reward patience! Choose what God chooses and exalt what God exalts!

VICTORY SECRET NO.19

The Secret of Heaven's Opinion

And unto the angel of the church in Sardis write; these things saith he that hath the seven Spirits of God, and the seven stars; I know thy works, that THOU HAST A NAME THAT THOU LIVEST, AND ART DEAD.

Be watchful, and strengthen the things which remain, that are ready to die: FOR I HAVE NOT FOUND THY WORKS PERFECT BEFORE GOD.

Remember therefore how thou hast received and heard, and hold fast, and repent. If therefore thou shalt not watch, I will come on thee as a thief, and thou shalt not know what hour I will come upon thee.

Revelation 3:1-3

The book of Revelation unveils things that are hidden from our view. Things that are not public knowledge are made known to us if we care to accept them.

Revelation means to unveil and to show something that is hidden.

The scripture above reveals God's assessment of the church in Sardis. God says, "You are a dead church."

What is Heaven's opinion about you? What is earth's opinion about you? Which one really matters? What God thinks about you is what is important. Most Christians do not have much discernment. Most of us are impressed with outward appearances. The church may look good and impressive, but God may not be impressed at all.

The scripture above shows that God may have an impression about you that is the exact opposite of what people think about you. In this case, people thought the church of Sardis was alive but God considered it to be a dead church. Men may think you are perfect; but if God does not find your works perfect then you are in big trouble.

What a terrible thing for God to declare you dead even though people say you are perfect! What a disaster for you to have a name that you are alive when you are actually dead!

Where did you get that name or reputation of being alive from? It is an impression that men have about you. People may praise you and extol your great works but God is not impressed.

The message to the church of Sardis is simple: Heaven is not impressed with you! Heaven considers you to be in the worst state possible. Heaven considers you dead! All the awards and congratulations you receive from men on this earth cannot change God's opinion about you.

Deception is the blanket under which the world lives. Even in the church world, people believe that the loudest church is the biggest and best church. Spurious ministers are often given glorious awards by men. (Spurious means not genuine and not authentic). Most people believe what they see on television and hear on the radio. Because of this, many shallow, empty and spurious things are acclaimed as the greatest and most important.

Do not follow the masses who are impressed with the fake, the deceptive and the artificial. Think of God and His Word. Think of God's standards. God sees through all our masks and pretences. Think of this church in Sardis that had such a good reputation with the world and yet had a very bad reputation in Heaven. Everyone on earth praised Sardis for being perfect. However everyone in Heaven could see that Sardis was dead. That is frightening! What does God really think about you and me? Take a little time to find out God's real opinion about you. Do not be over-confident. Be real! Be humble and accept God's standards so that you will not have a big shock when you see Him face to face.

VICTORY SECRET NO.20

The Secret of the Mid-Stream Corrections

And unto the angel of the church in Sardis write; These things saith he that hath the seven Spirits of God, and the seven stars; I know thy works, that thou hast a name that thou livest, and art dead.

Be watchful, and strengthen the things which remain, that are ready to die: for I have not found thy works perfect before God.

REMEMBER THEREFORE HOW THOU HAST RECEIVED AND HEARD, AND HOLD FAST, AND REPENT. If therefore thou shalt not watch, I will come on thee as a thief, and thou shalt not know what hour I will come upon thee.

Revelation 3:1-3

Most ministries start out well, trying to achieve things for God. Those who come up after, often fall away from the ideals and standards of the pioneers. One day, I visited the home of John Wesley, the founder of the Methodist Church. As I was being taken on a tour of his house and the church, the tour guide mumbled under his breath, "All the things which John Wesley fought against have come back into the church again."

Obviously, the current leaders of that church were not following the ways and teachings of John Wesley. "I have not found thy works perfect" is what the Lord is saying to most of us today. There are four things we need to do if we are to come back on track. Every mid-stream correction has four stages. All these four stages have to do with taking you back to where you first began. Let us look at the four things the angel of the Lord prescribes for making a mid-stream correction.

1. Remember what you have received.

Remember therefore how thou hast *RECEIVED* ...

Revelation 3:3

Remembering what you have received from God is very important in staying on the right path. What has God given you? The gifts, the experiences, your background, the people, the apostles, the prophets and the prophecies He has given you, are your great anchor in staying on course with Him. The church of God has received much revelation through the years. We know so much more than the generations of the past and yet we do so little.

One day, I met with an executive leader of a huge church. He described how he attended executive meetings to discuss the leadership of the church. Their founder had left them with a great church and a great ministry. With the death of the founder, this new executive was trying to take the church forward into new heights. He mentioned one significant thing that struck me.

He said, "We use the minutes of the meetings we had with our founder years ago to guide us in what we are doing today."

This is exactly what the church of Sardis was asked to do. "Remember what you have received".

2.   Remember what you have heard.

Remember therefore how thou hast received and **_HEARD..._**

Revelation 3:3

To do a mid-stream correction, you must also remember what God has spoken to you about. In 1988, I heard a voice saying to me, "From today you can teach...". These words have guided my life and ministry up till now. It is important for me to remember what I heard on that fateful day in 1988. Those words mean a lot to me. Remembering them helps me to know what to do in the ministry. I must teach! I must preach! I must write! I must win souls!

Think about the messages you have heard. Think about the words that the Lord has spoken to you. Those are guideposts for your life! Do not set aside the words that God spoke to you when you were young.

God always does new things. God always leads us on. But the things we have heard and the things we have received will always stabilise and guide us in the ministry.

3.   Hold fast.

Remember therefore how thou hast received and **heard, and _HOLD FAST,..._**

Revelation 3:3

It is important to hold fast to the good things you are doing. Are you doing altar calls? That is a good thing! Are you holding camp meetings? That is a good thing! Are you still holding crusades? That is a good thing! Are you holding healing services? That is a good thing! Are you training leaders? That is a good thing! A sad reality is that pastors often drop the very things that are most important. Ministers often discard the very wisdom that made them great in ministry.

I encountered a great man of God who loved preaching about the Holy Spirit and the anointing. Unfortunately, this man of God began speaking more about prosperity than the anointing. Yet, he had attracted so much money into his ministry when he only spoke about the Holy Spirit. It seemed that he was not holding fast to the very thing that was the secret of his success.

On another occasion, I encountered a great man of God who had gone on a mission for many years into a far away country. He had enjoyed such success and support for his missionary work. Unfortunately, this great missionary was teaching mostly on the marketplace, the crossover ministry, economics, financial management and impacting the political landscape of cities. I asked him why he did not rather hold fast to the beauty of missionary work and saving souls. I wanted to know why he would not rather raise up more missionaries to go into the world. I wanted to know why he was more interested in raising up Christian economists, Christian businessmen and Christian politicians. He did not want to hold fast to the salvation message he had received. He did not hold fast to the message of going into all the world to preach the gospel. He had thrown it out of the boat and was teaching on "Christians in the marketplace". This is why the book of Revelation teaches us to "*hold fast.*"

Mid-stream correction involves holding fast to what God placed in your hand. I once sat on a plane with the pastor of a 12,000-member church with over one hundred branches. His ministry was the most prominent ministry in his country. The pastor told me that he was embarking on an MBA program in the United States. He did not want to hold onto his pastoral work. He wanted to be a politician.

This great man of God explained to me how he would impact his nation through politics, agriculture and a sound economy.

The next time I saw him, he had resigned from his church to start a political party. Amazingly, this pastor veered off into secular work after twenty years of powerful ministry. Sadly, the secular masses for which he was forsaking his church did not even vote for him.

Even though political work is important, I am sure that pastoral work is more important to God. Being a minister of God is the high calling. I am sure that it is important to hold fast to the original calling of preaching and teaching the Word of God. We must be careful of not holding fast to our calling. God is sending you a sound warning to hold fast! This is a midstream correction for you!

4.   Repent.

Remember therefore how thou hast received and heard, and hold fast, and REPENT ...

Revelation 3:3

Repentance means doing a "U-turn" in your life and ministry. Every servant of God must be capable of "U-turns". A "U-turn" makes you turn around completely!

Look around you today; you will quickly identify many churches that should do a "U-turn" right now. It is easy to see how many of us have gone astray into all kinds of pseudo-gospel ministries.

One day, I met a pastor of a huge ministry. His ministry had blessed so many people over the years. However, he seemed to mostly concentrate on the issue of finances. It made one wonder whether this pastor was an accountant, an economist, a banker, an investment analyst, a treasurer of a bank, a stockbroker or a businessman. Amazingly, he preached almost exclusively about money.

Pastors have to be careful about deviating from what they should emphasize. An error can be diagnosed by what you emphasize. Whilst we were in medical school, my friends and I prayed, we still believed in God. We always prayed in medical school when we needed to. However, emphasizing on prayer and Bible studies in a medical school would have been an error. In medical school, we have to emphasize subjects like anatomy, physiology, biochemistry, internal medicine, paediatrics, ophthalmology, orthopaedics, surgery and psychiatry. These are the subjects that are emphasized in a medical school.

In a church, we must equally emphasize the Word of God, the gospel of Jesus Christ, the blood of Jesus, the resurrection, salvation, eternity, discipleship and the Holy Spirit. It is erroneous to emphasize business management, stock broking, investment analysis, finance management, taxation and politics in the church. A brief mention of these will do, but in a church none of these things can become the main thing. Turn around, my friend. Stop deceiving yourself. The fact that many people listen to you does not mean that you are right. You may think you are alive, but God sees you as dead.

It is important for us to repent from the error of wrong emphases and correct ourselves mid-stream!

The Secret of the Servants in the Temple

And one of the elders answered, saying unto me, What are these which are arrayed in white robes? and whence came they? And I said unto him, Sir, thou knowest. And he said to me, These are they which came out of great tribulation, and have washed their robes, and made them white in the blood of the Lamb.

THEREFORE ARE THEY BEFORE THE THRONE OF GOD, AND SERVE HIM DAY AND NIGHT IN HIS TEMPLE: and he that sitteth on the throne shall dwell among them. They shall hunger no more, neither thirst any more; neither shall the sun light on them, nor any heat. For the Lamb which is in the midst of the throne shall feed them, and shall lead them unto living fountains of waters: and God shall wipe away all tears from their eyes.

Revelation 7:13-17

In the book of Revelation, we have a wonderful picture of people serving in the temple of God. This vision shows us what it really means to serve the Lord. Read it for yourself and be amazed at the benefits of being a servant of the Lord.

One of the greatest blessings of serving God is the blessing of being looked after by the Lord Himself. Serving God totally, in the house of God, results in your being totally looked after by the Lamb.

The great blessing of serving the Lord cannot be compared with any other kind of service to any organization or person. What are the blessings of working all the time in the temple of the Lord?

David said, "One thing have I desired of the Lord, that will I seek after; that I may dwell in the house of the Lord all the days of my life, to behold the beauty of the Lord, and to enquire in his temple" (Psalm 27:4). Today, you can serve in the House of God. You do not have to get to Heaven to serve in His temple. You can serve Him right now. When you serve the Lord, you will be in the midst of His temple. As you serve God in the temple, expect seven wonderful rewards.

Seven Benefits of Serving in the Temple

1. As you serve God, you will never be hungry. You will never lack food till you die.

They shall HUNGER NO MORE, neither thirst any more; neither shall the sun light on them, nor any heat.

Revelation 7:16

2. As you serve God, you will never be thirsty. You will never be thirsty or uncomfortable till you die. You will always have drinks in your house. You will be able to serve your visitors with all kinds of drinks.

They shall hunger no more, NEITHER THIRST ANY MORE; neither shall the sun light on them, nor any heat.

Revelation 7:16

3. As you serve God, you will not be smitten by the sun. You will not be destroyed by the sunshine. You will have a house and a car to protect you from the direct sunshine. I once had a vision of three lay pastors, labouring in the sun and heat. The Holy Spirit told me that these pastors were labouring in the secular world, when they should be in the House of God. I called each one of them and invited them to come over into the temple and serve God Himself. Unfortunately, one of them opted to continue in the sun and heat where he remains until this day.

They shall hunger no more, neither thirst any more; NEITHER SHALL THE SUN LIGHT ON THEM, nor any heat.

Revelation 7:16

4. As you serve God, you will not feel hot and sweaty any more. You will no longer sweat in the day or in the night. Expect God to make you comfortable as you serve Him. Expect to have air conditioners cooling your environment all the time. God will give you enough money to buy a generator, a fan and an air conditioner.

They shall hunger no more, neither thirst any more; neither shall the sun light on them, NOR ANY HEAT.

Revelation 7:16

5. As you serve God, He will feed you. Expect God to feed you Himself. You will be pampered and loved because you served the Lord. God could have simply removed hunger from your life. But He decided to feed you Himself. This shows the extent to which God wants to rub you and pamper you. Expect to be pampered by the Lord.

For THE LAMB which is in the midst of the throne SHALL FEED THEM, and shall lead them unto living fountains of waters: and God shall wipe away all tears from their eyes.

Revelation 7:17

6. As you serve God, you will not lack direction. You will be brought to living fountains of water. All over the world, people go to beaches to experience the fun and thrill of the oceans. Living water creates such an exhilarating feeling. You have been promised an everlasting holiday with living fountains of waters spraying all over you just because you are serving the Lord. I feel sorry for people who think that serving the Lord is boring.

For THE LAMB which is in the midst of the throne shall feed them, and SHALL LEAD THEM UNTO LIVING FOUNTAINS of waters: and God shall wipe away all tears from their eyes.

Revelation 7:17

7. As you serve God, He will remove your sorrow and tears. Life on this earth is punctuated by tears, grief and sorrow. Serving in His temple is marked by the notable absence of sorrowful tears. You will cry no more when you serve the Lord.

For the Lamb which is in the midst of the throne shall feed them, and shall lead them unto living fountains of waters: and GOD SHALL WIPE AWAY ALL TEARS FROM THEIR EYES.

Revelation 7:17

VICTORY SECRET NO.22

The Secret of
the Prevailing Lion

And one of the elders saith unto me, weep not: behold,
**THE LION OF THE TRIBE OF JUDA, THE ROOT
OF DAVID, HATH PREVAILED** to open the book, and
to loose the seven seals thereof.

And I beheld, and, lo, in the midst of the throne and
of the four beasts, and in the midst of the elders, stood
a Lamb as it had been slain, having seven horns and
seven eyes, which are the seven Spirits of God sent
forth into all the earth. And he came and took the book
out of the right hand of him that sat upon the throne.

Revelation 5:5-7

The secret of the Lion of Judah is the secret of prevailing! To prevail is the ability to do two things: the ability "to be victorious" and the ability "to maintain your cause". A prevailing lion is a fighting lion. A prevailing lion is a lion that does not go back or change its direction. To become a prevailing lion, you must be a winner of many fights, battles and duels.

To be a prevailing lion is to become a fighter, a winner and a person who has defeated many others. You will have to defeat a number of things in order to receive the greatest rewards. Do not be sad at the number of fights you have on your hands. It is the fights, battles and challenges that give you the right to the rewards of God.

Fight the internal battles for your soul.

Defeat the enemies that fight you in your church.

Defeat the rebels! Maintain your stance!

Defeat the lethargy in Christians!

Defeat the financial opposition to your ministry.

Defeat the marital challenges that strangulate you.

To maintain your cause is to tirelessly and consistently press on in the will of God.

Maintain the message!

Maintain the calling to teach the word! Do not turn aside into vain jangling!

Maintain the levels of anointing!

Maintain the zeal! Do not let other lukewarm Christians make you feel that you are extreme.

I remember arriving in South America after a twenty-four hour journey. I met a brother who asked what I was doing there. I explained that I was there to preach for two days. He exclaimed,

"You travelled all this way just to preach for two days?" I almost felt silly for going there. I realized that Christians can turn you away from zealously serving God. It is Christians who can pass comments and make you feel foolish for loving and serving God.

People will ask, "Why are you fasting? Why have you gone to Africa? Why are you going to all these places? Why are you giving away all these books? Why are you not resting?"

Someone told me that serving in my church was too stressful and too much hard work. This brother decided to join a less stressful church where he would not feel the pressure to work for God.

Such people make you feel bad for working for the Lord. But I want to be like the Lion of Judah who prevailed and maintained his cause. I want to maintain my stance! I maintain that working for the Lord is the best thing to do.

I love serving the Lord! I like God! I like His work! I cannot be tired serving the Lord!

I love following the Lord!

I love being near the Lord and convincing people to love the Lord first!

The Secret of Being in the Spirit

I WAS IN THE SPIRIT ON THE LORD'S DAY, and heard behind me a great voice, as of a trumpet, Saying, I am Alpha and Omega, the first and the last: and, What thou seest, write in a book, and send it unto the seven churches which are in Asia; unto Ephesus, and unto Smyrna, and unto Pergamos, and unto Thyatira, and unto Sardis, and unto Philadelphia, and unto Laodicea.

Revelation 1:10-11

After this I looked, and, behold, a door was opened in heaven: and the first voice which I heard was as it were of a trumpet talking with me; which said, Come up hither, and I will shew thee things which must be hereafter. And **IMMEDIATELY I WAS IN THE SPIRIT:** and, behold, a throne was set in heaven, and one sat on the throne.

Revelation 4:1-2

J ohn was in the spirit on the Lord's day. I have always wondered what to do to be in the spirit. Why would I want to be in the spirit like John? When John was in the spirit he saw things that no eye has ever seen. Who would not want to be in the spirit and have a mighty revelation like John did?

John was in the spirit and he saw things that no eye has ever seen. It was simply being in the spirit on the Lord's Day that resulted in his seeing and hearing all these wonderful things. Today, if you want to also see such marvellous things you must somehow *be in the spirit.* Being in the spirit is a divinely-granted experience. No one can force himself to be in the spirit. However, you can decide to be spiritual, which is the next best thing to being in the spirit.

Most of us are in the flesh. Most of us are hardly ever spiritual. You must learn to become and to stay spiritual. *As you remain spiritual you can expect to actually enter the spirit.* To become spiritual and to stay spiritual you must simply avoid carnality. Carnality is well defined in the Bible. Carnality is the fleshly manifestation of the human being. Being carnal is the same as being non-spiritual. The flesh and the Spirit are contrary to each other. When you are in the flesh you are not in the Spirit and when you are in the Spirit you are not in the flesh.

For the flesh lusteth against the Spirit, and the Spirit against the flesh: and THESE ARE CONTRARY THE ONE TO THE OTHER: so that ye cannot do the things that ye would.

Galatians 5:17

The apostle Paul was able to identify unspiritual people very easily. As soon as he noticed envy, strife, confusion and division, he knew that he was dealing with an unspiritual bunch. They were carnal! Carnality is envy, strife, division, confusion and the like. To walk in the flesh is to be out of the spirit. To walk in the spirit is therefore to not walk in the flesh.

And I, brethren, could not speak unto you as unto spiritual, but as unto carnal, even as unto babes in Christ.

1 Corinthians 3:1

To walk in the spirit: It is to walk far away from adultery, fornication, uncleanness, lasciviousness, idolatry, witchcraft, hatred, variance, emulations, wrath, strife, seditions, heresies, envyings, murders, drunkenness and revellings.

To operate in the spirit: To operate in the spirit, speak in the spirit. Speaking in tongues is speaking in the spirit. Read it for yourself! Stay in the spirit by speaking in tongues. For he that speaketh in an unknown tongue speaketh not unto men, but unto God: for no man understandeth him; howbeit *in the spirit* he speaketh mysteries. (1 Corinthians 14:2).

To exit the spirit: All you need to do is to walk in adultery, fornication, uncleanness, lasciviousness, idolatry, witchcraft, hatred, variance, emulations, wrath, strife, seditions, heresies, envyings, murders, drunkenness and revellings.

The Secret of the Lost Crowns

Because thou hast kept the word of my patience, I also will keep thee from the hour of temptation, which shall come upon all the world, to try them that dwell upon the earth. Behold, I come quickly: **HOLD THAT FAST WHICH THOU HAST, THAT NO MAN TAKE THY CROWN.**

Revelation 3:10-11

Five Reasons Why Your Crown Can be Lost

1. You can lose your crown because of your casual attitude.

Not realising that you have a great thing can cause you to toy with your ministry. Be careful of being casual about your calling. Stop assuming that what you have will always be there. I remember a homeless lady who was given a place to stay in someone's home. She did not realise the privilege that she had and despised the great opportunity to live in that home. After a while, she lost her place and became homeless again. She soon began to beg for the opportunity to go back to her place, but it was gone. She lost her position because of her casual attitude towards her host.

How sad it is to lose your crown just because you did not realise that it was a great thing. Today, there are people who think to themselves, "I don't need a crown in Heaven, I need a car on earth!" One day, many people are going to wish they had a crown. They will realise how unimportant a car was. You will wish you had been more serious about the calling.

2. You can lose your crown because you do not become strong.

There is a reason why God says be strong in the Lord. Not being good and strong in what you are doing is very dangerous. When you do not improve yourself in what you are doing you are in danger of a stronger person displacing you.

When a strong man armed keepeth his palace, his goods are in peace: BUT WHEN A STRONGER THAN HE shall come upon him, and overcome him, he taketh from him all his armour wherein he trusted, and divideth his spoils.

Luke 11:21-22

I remember encouraging musicians and singers to develop themselves and improve their skills. Unfortunately, many of them did not believe what I was saying and were soon replaced by stronger singers and musicians. Dear friend, it is important to be strong and well-developed in what you are doing. Always remember that others are strengthening themselves, hoping to displace you soon.

3.   Chasing fantasies can cause you to lose your crown.

He who works his land will have abundant food, but the one who chases fantasies will have his fill of poverty...

Proverbs 28:19 (NIV)

Many people have laid aside the call of God and are chasing imaginary prosperity. When God puts something substantial in your hand, do not let it go to chase after fantasies, lest you come to poverty. I once gave someone a job but he despised the job, thinking that there were other greater things that he could do.

He decided to go into business. I watched him doing his business every day, waiting to see signs of prosperity. Unfortunately, the signs of prosperity simply did not come. Eventually, when all hope was lost, he decided to come back to what he originally had in his hands. Through the job that I gave him, he was blessed much more than when he was into his business. Often, people lay aside what is real and follow fantasies. The Bible is clear that such things always lead to poverty.

In the same way, ministers have laid aside the call of God and have gone chasing fantasies. This will only cause them to lose their crowns. On earth no one may notice that you have swerved aside into useless pursuits. God sees us chasing fantasies all the time.

4.   Resting and relaxing can cause you to lose your crown.

But while men slept, his enemy came and sowed tares among the wheat, and went his way.

Matthew 13:25

There is a time to work and there is a time to rest. Whilst we are on this earth it is time to work. If you rest when you should not be resting, the enemy will come in and sow destruction in the midst of your good seeds. It is time to wake, O sleeper! You may lose your crown because you love resting when you should be working.

5. Jezebel can cause you to lose your crown.

Then Jezebel sent a messenger unto Elijah, saying, so let the gods do to me, and more also, if I make not thy life as the life of one of them by to morrow about this time. And when he saw that, he arose, and went for his life, and came to Beersheba, which belongeth to Judah, and left his servant there.

1 Kings 19:2-3

Elijah lost his place through the manipulations of Jezebel. Jezebel is the ultimate evil woman that you do not want to meet. Through her manipulation, comments, negative advice and negative comments you can be completely derailed from your life's mission.

Elijah was not afraid of four hundred false prophets of Baal but he ran away from Jezebel. This should show you the power of Jezebel to make you lose your crown.

When a man unfortunately marries a Jezebel, he may be steered into doing the wrong thing. He may be pushed and pulled until he decides to abandon his calling. Many ministers of God are married to Jezebel queens.

Many pastors are unable to stand up to the Jezebel spirit that dominates their home. Jezebel is the profound and ultimate manipulator, commentator, advisor who is anointed with jealousy and hatred. She stands at the back and influences everyone without them realising what is happening.

Remember that Ahab would never have killed Naboth. It was Jezebel who advised Ahab to use his powers as a king to get rid of Naboth. It was Jezebel who organised worthless fellows to kill Naboth. No one ever saw her killing Naboth, but she was a murderer and she was filled with hatred.

It is a pitiful sight to see some husbands humbly following their own personal Jezebel into fruitlessness and emptiness. It is a sorry sight to see men who are emasculated, dominated and cowered into submission by a Jezebel.

It is sad that some people use Bible verses wrongly. Misapplying scripture allows Jezebels to be even more empowered. "Husbands, love your wives", they say. A Jezebel is not a normal wife. A Jezebel is a Jezebel. "Love your Jezebel. Let her do what she wants. It is a short life. You must have peace", is not in the scriptures. What scripture does say about Jezebel is clear. Don't allow her to manoeuvre. Don't allow the Jezebelic manipulator, commentator and advisor to have power in the church.

Notwithstanding I have a few things against thee, because thou sufferest that woman Jezebel, which calleth herself a prophetess, to teach and to seduce my servants to commit fornication, and to eat things sacrificed unto idols.

Revelation 2:20

The Secret of the Mysteries of God

And the angel which I saw stand upon the sea and upon the earth lifted up his hand to heaven, and sware by him that liveth for ever and ever, who created heaven, and the things that therein are, and the earth, and the things that therein are, and the sea, and the things which are therein, that there should be time no longer.

But in the days of the voice of the seventh angel, when he shall begin to sound, THE MYSTERY OF GOD SHOULD BE FINISHED, as he hath declared to his servants the prophets.

Revelation 10:5-7

This is a great prophecy. The mystery of God will be finished in the days of the voice of the seventh angel. God will answer all our questions and solve all the mysteries that surround us. God will explain everything that disturbed us and confused us whilst we served Him here below. This promise will take place in the days of the voice of the seventh angel.

God is a God of mystery and He has no apologies for that!

There are many illogical events, mysterious happenings and mysterious realities in our world today. Mystery is part of our lives on this earth. We try to serve God but we constantly experience things that defy our understanding.

God does not follow our logic! God does not do what we expect! God does not owe us explanations! We are nothing! Even within the universe the earth is but a dot in the sky!

God does not think the way we think. Many things about God are not clear. Often, the way we want things to turn out are not the way God will do them.

You will make many mistakes when you ignore the mysterious nature of God. God is mysterious! You cannot discount the mysteries of God.

The reason why God and His ways seem so mysterious to us is because our thoughts are vastly different from His thoughts. So many things God does are mysterious to us. Indeed our ways and thoughts are far – very far, from God's ways.

"For My thoughts are not your thoughts, nor are your ways My ways", declares the Lord.

For as the heavens are higher than the earth, so are My ways higher than your ways and My thoughts than your thoughts.

Isaiah 55:8-9 (NASB)

The great prophecy of the seventh angel marks the ending of this mystery that surrounds God. At the voice of the seventh angel, a new and a far greater understanding of God will be born. Until then, you cannot live without accepting the mystery of God and humbling yourself under His mighty hand.

When you do not flow with this reality that God is a mysterious God who has no intention of revealing everything to us, you will make catastrophic mistakes in your life and ministry. You will make mistakes in your predictions, expectations, hopes, preaching and teaching. You will be strong and adamant about certain points when you should have been humble and open to the mysteries of God. You may even preach that you will live forever and never die, only to die in the midst of your years. These are some of the common mistakes we make when we do not want to accept the mysteries of God.

Before the seventh angel blows his trumpet, do not expect life to follow a logical trend. Expect mysterious events to spring up questions along your entire journey with the Lord.

What Happens When You Do Not Consider the Mysteries of God

1. When you don't carefully consider the mysteries of God, you will predict outcomes that will not happen. You will make declarations about the future that will never come to pass. You will only predict good things when evil things are about to happen. You may think that God works with your logic, but He does not.

   Who is he that saith, and it cometh to pass, when the Lord commandeth it not?

   Lamentations 3:37

   When you don't carefully consider the mysteries of God, your expectations are cut off time and time and again. When you don't carefully consider the mystery of God, you look like a fool because you told people what God would do but

God did not do it. When you don't carefully consider the mystery of God, you preach with arrogance and pride that will painfully be corrected in you. When you don't carefully consider the mystery of God, you cannot understand the commandments of God since they don't make logical sense to you.

2. When you don't carefully consider the mysteries of God, you will explain things you do not really understand. You will explain why certain people died untimely deaths. When you don't carefully consider the mystery of God, you will give reasons for why certain things have happened. Like Job's friends, you will offer wrong reasons for tragedies and calamities that have taken place.

And it was so, that after the Lord had spoken these words unto Job, the Lord said to Eliphaz the Temanite, My wrath is kindled against thee, and against thy two friends: for ye have not spoken of me the thing that is right, as my servant Job hath.

Job 42:7

3. When you don't carefully consider the mysteries of God, you will condemn things that God has not condemned. You will consider certain men of God to have fallen out of God's approval only to discover them sitting on royal thrones in Heaven.

Who art thou that judgest another man's servant? to his own master he standeth or falleth. Yea, he shall be holden up: for God is able to make him stand.

Romans 14:4

4. When you don't carefully consider the mysteries of God, you will approve of things God does not approve of. Like Samuel, you will approve of people when they look good on the outward. You will not understand why God chooses certain people and uses them for mighty works. In your estimation, God should not choose certain people whom

you despise. Mysteriously, God chose David, a young outcast of the family of Jesse and rejected his older, tall and handsome brothers.

But the Lord said unto Samuel, Look not on his countenance, or on the height of his stature; because I have refused him: for the Lord seeth not as man seeth; for man looketh on the outward appearance, but the Lord looketh on the heart.

1 Samuel 16:7

5. When you don't carefully consider the mysteries of God, you will be disappointed and broken hearted and depressed when you should not be. The people who followed Jesus to the cross were broken-hearted and disappointed at the way their Saviour was being treated. They could not understand the great mystery that was unfolding.

And there followed him a great company of people, and of women, which also bewailed and lamented him.

But Jesus turning unto them said, Daughters of Jerusalem, weep not for me, but weep for yourselves, and for your children. For, behold, the days are coming, in the which they shall say, Blessed are the barren, and the wombs that never bare, and the paps which never gave suck.

Then shall they begin to say to the mountains, Fall on us; and to the hills, Cover us. For if they do these things in a green tree, what shall be done in the dry?

Luke 23:27-31

6. When you don't carefully consider the mystery of God, you prepare for things wrongly. You may be preparing for a long life when you should be preparing for death. Mysteriously, God may want you to die instead of living longer. Jesus, the Son of God, died at the age of thirty-three. John the Baptist died at thirty. To men, it is puzzling but that is the mystery of God.

7. When you don't carefully consider the mysteries of God, you battle with the instructions of God all the time and disobey many of them. Saul could not understand the instructions to kill everyone including king Agag, the women, the children and the animals from Amalek. God is mysterious and you must respect that mystery!

Then came the word of the Lord unto Samuel, saying, It repenteth me that I have set up Saul to be king: for he is turned back from following me, and hath not performed my commandments. And it grieved Samuel; and he cried unto the Lord all night.

1 Samuel 15:10-11

8. When you don't carefully consider the mysteries of God, you have a wrong understanding of love and kindness. You will even have a wrong definition of good and evil. You will wrestle with scriptures like the one below. "How can God create evil?" you will ask. You will even attempt to be kinder than God.

I form the light, and create darkness: I make peace, and create evil: I the Lord do all these things.

Isaiah 45:7

9. When you don't carefully consider the mysteries of God, you have a wrong definition of good and evil. Like Adam and Eve, you will want your own definition of what is right or wrong. Setting aside the mysterious will of God and trying to do your own thing will lead to much evil.

And the Lord God commanded the man, saying, Of every tree of the garden thou mayest freely eat: But of the tree of the knowledge of good and evil, thou shalt not eat of it: for in the day that thou eatest thereof thou shalt surely die.

Genesis 2:16-17

10. When you don't carefully consider the mysteries of God, you will make wrong judgments about people's marriages. In the Old Testament, the Bible seems to accept the concept of polygamy. Abraham, Isaac, Jacob, David, Solomon and all the kings of Israel were polygamists.

    God is against divorce and adultery in both the Old Testament and the New Testament. All through the Old Testament, God showed His anger against idolatry. Yet He never commented about their polygamy. This is indeed a mystery. What exactly is God's mind about marriage?

11. When you don't carefully consider the mysteries of God, you may pass the wrong judgment on people who are divorced. You will find that God hates divorce and yet He himself declares that He has divorced Israel.

    Thus says the Lord, Where is the certificate of divorce by which I have sent your mother away?

    Or to whom of my creditors did I sell you? Behold, you were sold for your iniquities, and for your transgressions your mother was sent away.

    Isaiah 50:1 (NASB)

12. When you don't carefully consider the mysteries of God, you may abandon God and forsake the Word of God. This is what has happened to most Europeans. They cannot understand a mysterious God. The whole of Europe has forsaken God because they cannot understand the mysteries of God.

The Secret of
the Seventh Angel

And the angel which I saw stand upon the sea and upon the earth lifted up his hand to heaven, and sware by him that liveth for ever and ever, who created heaven, and the things that therein are, and the earth, and the things that therein are, and the sea, and the things which are therein, that there should be time no longer.

BUT IN THE DAYS OF THE VOICE OF THE SEVENTH ANGEL, WHEN HE SHALL BEGIN TO SOUND, THE MYSTERY OF GOD SHOULD BE FINISHED, as he hath declared to his servants the prophets.

Revelation 10:5-7

AND THE SEVENTH ANGEL SOUNDED; AND THERE WERE GREAT VOICES IN HEAVEN, SAYING, THE KINGDOMS OF THIS WORLD ARE BECOME THE KINGDOMS OF OUR LORD, and of his Christ; and he shall reign for ever and ever. And the four and twenty elders, which sat before God on their seats, fell upon their faces, and worshipped God, saying, We give thee thanks, O Lord God Almighty, which art, and wast, and art to come; because thou hast taken to thee thy great power, and hast reigned.

Revelation 11:15-17

I t is the seventh angel that our world awaits.

The book of Revelation clearly unveils things that are hidden from our view. Things that are not public knowledge are made known to us if we care to accept them.

Revelation means to unveil and to show something that is hidden.

In the book of Revelation, we see the seventh angel sounding his trumpet. This sparks off the changes which all of humanity have been waiting for. When you understand the events that are sparked off by this angel, your heart will be at rest in this chaotic world.

The confusion in this world will be brought to an abrupt end by the seventh angel. Why is this? Note the events that are triggered off by this angel.

1.   **When the seventh angel sounds, the kingdoms of this world will become the kingdoms of Jesus Christ.**

And the seventh angel sounded; and there were great voices in heaven, saying, the kingdoms of this world are become the kingdoms of our Lord, and of his Christ; and he shall reign for ever and ever.

Revelation 11:15

The seventh angel will sound his trumpet and the nations of this world will become the nations under Jesus Christ. Today, the kingdoms of this world are *not* the kingdoms of our Lord. There is no point in declaring different nations as Christian countries. It is a waste of your time. The kingdoms of this world are securely under the governments of the god of the world, which is the devil himself.

This accounts for the ever-increasing entropy and confusion everywhere. It also accounts for the increasing number of nations that are now under the rule of violent and intolerant religions.

2.   When the seventh angel sounds, Jesus will begin to reign forever and ever.

The seventh angel will sound his trumpet and Jesus will reign forever and ever. From this point onwards, there will be no more democracy in the world.

Democracy is one of the most inadequate systems of government ever used by men. It is fraught with the weaknesses of deception, corruption and fraud. Entire nations are led by men who could never even lead a small company. Democracy has caused nations to be ruled by inadequate men who have never worked or built anything. Corrupt, lying and violent men are set up as democratic leaders everywhere because of this failing human system. The seventh angel will put an end to this nonsense!

There will also be no more royal families, kings, chiefs and traditional leaders who influence nations, leaving the masses with little or nothing to go by. The opulent and vain ruling dynasties of this world will be gone forever. We will never be tormented by the likes of King Henry VIII or some of the African chiefs of old who have ruled their people in poverty for centuries.

3.   When the seventh angel sounds, Jesus will begin to exert His power and authority at last.

And the four and twenty elders, which sat before God on their seats, fell upon their faces, and worshipped God, Saying, We give thee thanks, O Lord God Almighty, which art, and wast, and art to come; because THOU HAST TAKEN TO THEE THY GREAT POWER, AND HAST REIGNED.

Revelation 11:16-17

The seventh angel will sound his trumpet and Jesus will take His great authority and rule the world. What we do not realize is that we have been living in a world where God has not exerted His great authority and power. This world has been allowed to go on without God stepping in or intervening much. It is the prayers of the saints that have led to God's intervention on certain occasions.

Hardly has God said anything when men have said that He (God) does not exist. God said nothing when scientists made discoveries of planets and galaxies only to declare that there is no God. God was silent on all these issues. He has made no comment to the scientists and inventors of this world.

God has not intervened as men have fought one another and killed millions meaninglessly. God has not intervened when we have used money to manufacture weapons rather than solve the problems of this world.

God did not intervene when His Son was crucified on the cross. He allowed wicked men to do whatever they wanted.

God did not intervene when Christians were persecuted all over the world. God did not intervene when Jews were slaughtered for centuries.

God has not intervened as false religions have taken over nations and killed thousands.

Where is God in all this? It is a great mystery. The silence of God has been the greatest mystery of all time.

But I assure you that, in the days of the seventh angel, this mystery will be over for good. The mystery of God will be solved in the day of the seventh angel.

But in the days of the voice of the seventh angel, when he shall begin to sound, THE MYSTERY OF GOD SHOULD BE FINISHED, as he hath declared to his servants the prophets.

Revelation 10:7

God will use His great power and exert it in a way that the whole world will see and fear the reality and awesomeness of a living God.

4.   **When the seventh angel sounds, the nations will be angry at God's takeover.**

And THE NATIONS WERE ANGRY, and thy wrath is come, and the time of the dead, that they should be judged, and that thou shouldest give reward unto thy servants the prophets, and to the saints, and them that fear thy name, small and great; and shouldest destroy them which destroy the earth.

Revelation 11:18

The seventh angel will sound his trumpet and the nations of this world will be angry at the take-over of Jesus Christ. The nations of this world will reject the takeover by the Lord Jesus and His great power. But they will be powerless because God Himself will subdue this wicked world. Like with most prisoners and criminals, the world will have to be dealt with by force. The world is full of rebellious men who do not acknowledge God. Even when they do acknowledge God it is for their selfish, financial or political reasons.

5.   **When the seventh angel sounds, the rewards for the prophets, saints and servants of God will be given out.**

And the nations were angry, and thy wrath is come, and the time of the dead, that they should be judged, and that thou shouldest GIVE REWARD UNTO THY SERVANTS THE PROPHETS, AND TO THE SAINTS, and them that fear thy name, small and great; and shouldest destroy them which destroy the earth.

Revelation 11:18

The seventh angel will sound his trumpet and rewards will be given to the servants, the prophets and saints of God. All those who have served God will be glad they did. On that day, the believers in Jesus and the true Christians will be the happiest. They will be glad for every day, every moment and every second they spent in the service of the King.

6. **When the seventh angel sounds, those who destroy the earth will be destroyed.**

    And the nations were angry, and thy wrath is come, and the time of the dead, that they should be judged, and that thou shouldest give reward unto thy servants the prophets, and to the saints, and them that fear thy name, small and great; and shouldest DESTROY THEM WHICH DESTROY THE EARTH.

    Revelation 11:18

The seventh angel will sound his trumpet and those who destroyed the earth will be destroyed. Why God allows the earth to be destroyed by men is another mystery we are yet to understand. But we do know for sure that in the day of the seventh angel, the nonsensical leadership of mankind, which only leads to war and destruction, will be finally over. The world we live in is being destroyed slowly but very surely! You just have to watch a secular government at work and you will see the destruction they unleash into this world.

It is important to know the overall plan of God and to console yourself in the fact that God is aware that nations are being systematically destroyed by men. Imagine heads of state travelling all over the world to coerce nations to accept that two men can and should marry. You wonder why state money and power should be used to propagate homosexuality in the world! Is it not an agenda to destroy the human race with perversions? Imagine having presidents of rich countries bullying poor nations to accept homosexuality. The destruction of our world through politics is amazing!

Most decisions are taken because they are good politically and not because they will really help the nation. A world full of greedy, selfish, wicked, deceptive and corrupt leaders is only headed towards doomsday.

Many nations have leaders who systematically destroy their countries through their bad decisions. You can see the destruction best in the currencies of poor countries. These nations may cook up deceptive economic figures but the constant devaluation of their currencies reveal the ineptitude of the leaders. As the currencies of poor countries are helplessly devalued, the incompetence, arrogance and absurd policies of the managers of the nation are revealed.

Pastors must not try to take political power over nations. The church should not try to do the work of the seventh angel. This is why God has not called pastors to do the work of politics. God does not need more politicians. God needs more pastors. God needs more prophets. God needs more evangelists. In the day of the seventh angel, all the political problems will be solved.

Politics cannot do more than the church can do. Politics achieves very little. Even those in political power realize that they can't do very much. Some politicians may even agree that the country is worse off after their term in office.

Let us preach the gospel! As many as believe and are saved are blessed indeed! The total transformation of this world into the kingdoms of Christ will take place only in the days of the seventh angel!

You may wrestle with the confusion in the world today; but it is only in the days of the seventh angel that the confusion in our world will end.

The Secret of Spiritual Identity

And there was given me a reed like unto a rod: and the angel stood, saying, Rise, and measure the temple of God, and the altar, and them that worship therein. But the court which is without the temple leave out, and measure it not; for it is given unto the Gentiles: and the holy city shall they tread under foot forty and two months.

And I will give power unto my two witnesses, and they shall prophesy a thousand two hundred and threescore days, clothed in sackcloth.

These are the two olive trees, and the two candlesticks standing before the God of the earth. And if any man will hurt them, fire proceedeth out of their mouth, and devoureth their enemies: and if any man will hurt them, he must in this manner be killed. These have power to shut heaven, that it rain not in the days of their prophecy: and have power over waters to turn them to blood, and to smite the earth with all plagues, as often as they will.

And when they shall have finished their testimony, the beast that ascendeth out of the bottomless pit shall make war against them, and shall overcome them, and kill them. AND THEIR DEAD BODIES SHALL LIE

IN THE STREET OF THE GREAT CITY, WHICH SPIRITUALLY IS CALLED SODOM AND EGYPT, WHERE ALSO OUR LORD WAS CRUCIFIED. And they of the people and kindreds and tongues and nations shall see their dead bodies three days and an half, and shall not suffer their dead bodies to be put in graves.

Revelation 11:1-9

Jerusalem is known as the holy mountain of God and the seat of David. But in the book of Revelation a whole new identity of Jerusalem is unveiled. Jerusalem is actually called Sodom (the city destined for destruction) and Egypt (the nation destined for the plagues and judgments of God). Think about that! Jerusalem, the holy city that we make pilgrimages to, is spiritually called by the damned name "Sodom"! Imagine that Jerusalem can also be spiritually called "Egypt"! What are you called spiritually?

> **Wherefore henceforth know we no man after the flesh: yea, though we have known Christ after the flesh, yet now henceforth know we him no more.**
>
> **2 Corinthians 5:16**

Everyone has a spiritual identity apart from his known physical identity. This is what Paul meant when he said he does not know or relate with people after the flesh. Paul dealt with people by what they were called spiritually. You must begin to ask God for the true spiritual identity of the people you are encountering in your life. If you do not know whom you are dealing with, how will you know how to behave?

Not knowing a person's spiritual identity can make you reject the very person you need in your life. For instance, if someone is spiritually your "father" and you reject him, you will lose all the inheritance that you could have had. If a person is spiritually your father, and you dishonour him, you will bring upon yourself a curse. If you dishonour someone who is not spiritually your father, nothing bad will happen to you. It is important to recognize everyone's spiritual identity.

Spiritual Identities

1. **The spiritual identity of the Nazarene carpenter:** Jesus' spiritual identity was the Messiah. Jesus wanted Peter to know the spiritual identity of his Lord and Messiah! Do you know that the identity of a person could be vastly different from what you even imagine?

And Simon Peter answered and said, Thou art the Christ, the Son of the living God.

Matthew 16:16

2. **The spiritual identity of Mary's baby:** The son of Mary was spiritually called the Christ, the Son of God. In the natural, everyone would have called Jesus the son of Mary and Joseph. Spiritually, He was called Christ.

For unto you is born this day in the city of David a Saviour, which is Christ the Lord.

Luke 2:11

3. **The spiritual identity of John the Baptist:** John the Baptist was actually Elijah.

And if ye will receive it, this is Elias, which was for to come.

Matthew 11:14

4. **The spiritual identity of the disciples:** Those who heard and obeyed Christ's message were spiritually called the brothers, sisters and mother of Jesus.

But he answered and said unto him that told him, Who is my mother? and who are my brethren?

Matthew 12:48

5. **The spiritual identity of Elijah:** Elijah's spiritual identity was the father of Elisha.

And Elisha saw it, and he cried, My father, my father, the chariot of Israel, and the horsemen thereof. And he saw him no more: and he took hold of his own clothes, and rent them in two pieces.

2 Kings 2:12

Perhaps you have met someone who is spiritually called Absalom!

Perhaps you are encountering someone who is spiritually called Judas!

Perhaps you are encountering someone who is spiritually called your daughter!

Perhaps you are encountering someone who is spiritually called your son!

Perhaps you are encountering someone who is spiritually called your friend!

Perhaps you are encountering someone who is spiritually called your father!

Perhaps you are encountering someone who is spiritually called your mother! Seek for the spiritual identities of the people you relate with. Make sure you do not make a mistake.

VICTORY SECRET NO. 28

The Secret of the Red Dragon

And there appeared a great wonder in heaven; a woman clothed with the sun, and the moon under her feet, and upon her head a crown of twelve stars: And she being with child cried, travailing in birth, and pained to be delivered.

AND THERE APPEARED ANOTHER WONDER IN HEAVEN; AND BEHOLD A GREAT RED DRAGON, HAVING SEVEN HEADS AND TEN HORNS, AND SEVEN CROWNS UPON HIS HEADS. And his tail drew the third part of the stars of heaven, and did cast them to the earth: and THE DRAGON STOOD BEFORE THE WOMAN WHICH WAS READY TO BE DELIVERED, FOR TO DEVOUR HER CHILD AS SOON AS IT WAS BORN.

Revelation 12:1-4

The red dragon, which is the devil himself, is exposed in this passage as targeting the child and offspring of the "Wonder Woman" in Heaven. This "Wonder Woman" was to bring forth a man-child. The great red dragon had only one aim: to devour the child that she was to bring forth.

The focus of the red dragon is very revealing. *The child you bring forth: your fruits, your children, your disciples, your followers, your products are the most important works of your life and also the prime targets of an intelligent enemy.*

This intelligent onslaught of the red dragon on the most important aspects of your ministry should reveal to you what your focus must be.

This is the wisdom that Christ possessed. He did not seem to be interested much in ministering Himself. He lived and preached for only three years and depended on the twelve disciples to reach the world. He was focused on producing twelve people just like Himself.

Since the prime target of the red dragon is the man-child you bring forth, your strengths and efforts must be to produce the man-child and to preserve him. All true fruit-bearing ministries must be directed at producing offspring and *not* at ministering yourself.

You will notice that after the red dragon was unable to eliminate the prime target, he turned his attention to the other seeds and fruits of the "Wonder Woman". The seed and fruits of your ministry will always be the prime target of the devil.

And the dragon was wroth with the woman, and went to make WAR WITH THE REMNANT OF HER SEED, which keep the commandments of God, and have the testimony of Jesus Christ.

Revelation 12:17

The dragon will try hard to eliminate Bible schools. He will try hard to transform Bible schools into secular universities. He will try hard to make pastors set up great secular universities instead of setting up great ministry training centres. He will encourage pastors to promote the teaching of physics, economics, finance, chemistry and biology rather than promoting the teaching of the Word of God. The red dragon is at war with the seed. The red dragon wants to eliminate the seed of all ministers.

It is important for disciple-making to be the greatest investment of your ministry. I once asked a pastor to get his young men trained in a Bible school, but he would not. Unfortunately the church he pastored gradually shrunk, as he got older.

I asked another man of God to send his young men abroad for training in ministry. Sadly he did not see the importance of spending that amount of money on exposing his young people to a broader kind of training.

What are the products we must seek to release into the world? Why is the red dragon so intent on destroying the seed that is produced? Real ministry depends on you producing mighty offspring and disciples! I have seen seventy-year-old ministers who have to do the work of a thirty-year-old pastor because there are no young men who can do the work. The red dragon has devoured the seed of the woman.

Produce Lay People

We must invest heavily in the training of cell leaders, shepherds and lay church workers. There must always be schools that produce and release such trained workers.

Then we must invest heavily in producing lay or part time pastors. There must always be schools that produce and release lay and volunteer pastors.

Produce Missionaries

We must invest heavily in the training of full time missionaries. Many churches have no such program for the release of full time missionaries.

There must be long and short programs to produce ministers. There must not be a rigid system of producing pastors because only God knows those who are really called. Many who go through long rigid systems of pastoral training amount to nothing.

Produce Ministers as Fast as Possible

When John Wesley came on the scene, people were appalled at the ease with which he appointed new ministers. At one point his American director of the Methodist church, Francis Asbury came up with a short simple plan for ordaining pastors. This plan shocked the world; many were appalled with his easy way of appointing pastors. But that was the secret for the phenomenal growth of the Methodist Church in America.

Asbury's plan for ordination of pastors was simple: Ask four questions and if you get a positive response for all four questions, then ordain them.

Imagine that! Just ask four questions and if you get a positive response, ordain them. His four questions were:

1. Is this man truly converted?

2. Does he know and keep our rules?

3. Can he preach acceptably?

4. Has he a horse?

This simple system enabled him to release many pastors and itinerant ministers for the Methodist Church of America. Other institutions for preparing the clergy could not keep up with this fast paced ministry. The Methodist Church very quickly outgrew the established churches in number.

Preparation of people to become pastors must be flexible and must entertain an abundance of variations. It should take from as short as one day to as long as several years, for a person to become an accepted minister. Inflexible systems only lead to a decline in church growth.

Produce Bishops

We must also have a program for the training and developing of bishops and more senior clergy. The program for the training of bishops is completely different from the training of ordinary pastors. A bishop must be broad minded and able to deal with a broader variety of issues including international relations, governmental relations and many other secular issues. A bishop must be a permanent, lifetime and faithful fruit bearer. He must be a successful church builder.

Produce Helps Ministers

Then there must be a system for producing helps ministers. Musicians and quality singers must be consciously trained and released. Helpers who are honest, hardworking and productive must be trained by setting them to work on practical tasks in the church.

Financial helps ministers must also be released by encouraging business and secular workers to follow the principles of prosperity; which start by loving God, loving His house and serving Him whole heartedly.

Business leaders and helpers must be taught not to borrow money and not to follow the ways of the world that tend to poverty and financial crises.

The Secret of Keeping the Garments

Behold, I come as a thief. Blessed is he that watcheth, and KEEPETH HIS GARMENTS, lest he walk naked, and they see his shame.

Revelation 16:15

Nakedness is a reality for all who serve the Lord. Everyone is naked before putting on his clothes. A naked body lies unrevealed beneath each person's clothes. Amazingly, when unclothed, most people look a little less sharp and even appear to be a downgraded version of themselves!

You would have thought that nakedness is more attractive but it is usually not so. Shapelessness, big tummies, distorted figures, overweight bodies, thin lean skeletons, skinny legs, overgrown hair, white and grey hairs, disproportionate breasts, sagging breasts and other embarrassing organs are all hidden under the garments.

In the ministry, we all have nakedness too. This nakedness is not a sin. It is not a sin to have a naked body. But it is embarrassing for the real, weak, feeble and failing bodies that we have, to be revealed to all.

This is why you need to fight to keep your garments on. Garments speak of anything that protects you from having your weakness and nakedness becoming a source of embarrassment to you. Sickness, health problems, marital problems, financial problems, quarrels and human failures are all part of our nakedness.

Jesus had human realities and there were certain people who had the ability to handle those human realities and not be affected negatively. John the apostle was one such person. He said he had handled the Word of life. He declared that he had touched, seen, observed and related with the Word of life. He must have seen the nakedness (humanness) of Jesus. Yet he never turned against Jesus but rather spoke of His glory and greatness.

That which was from the beginning, which we have heard, which we have seen with our eyes, which we have looked upon, and our hands have handled, of the Word of life;

(For the life was manifested, and we have seen it, and bear witness, and shew unto you that eternal life, which was with the Father, and was manifested unto us;)

That which we have seen and heard declare we unto you, that ye also may have fellowship with us: and truly our fellowship is with the Father, and with his Son Jesus Christ.

1 John 1:1-3

Not everyone has this wonderful ability of seeing the nakedness and shame of God's servant and still believe in him.

I remember a man of God whose family was puzzled by their father's ability to pray for the sick while he himself struggled with cancer until he died. They could not fathom why their father could pray for people to be healed and yet not receive healing himself.

You must strive to cover up the humanness of your life and ministry by having helpers, people like John in your life. This John will be a covering to you. Much evil is determined against you when you are not careful about choosing the people who can dwell with you whilst observing your nakedness (humanness). People who do not have this gift develop the spirit of familiarity, pride and arrogance.

Being surrounded by those who have the gift of John the disciple is a great blessing. Jesus really loved John. When He was dying on the cross, He asked John to look after His mother. It was John He trusted with His human issues. Peter was nowhere to be found. John was experienced in handling the nakedness (humanness) of the Saviour. He could and would handle Jesus' mother very well. May God give you garments (helpers) that cover the nakedness, weakness, frailty and humanness of your life!

VICTORY SECRET NO. 30

The Secret of the Number of the Beast

And I saw another sign in heaven, great and marvellous, seven angels having the seven last plagues; for in them is filled up the wrath of God.

And I saw as it were a sea of glass mingled with fire: and **THEM THAT HAD GOTTEN THE VICTORY OVER THE BEAST, AND OVER HIS IMAGE, AND OVER HIS MARK, AND OVER THE NUMBER OF HIS NAME,** stand on the sea of glass, having the harps of God. And they sing the song of Moses the servant of God, and the song of the Lamb, saying, Great and marvellous are thy works, Lord God Almighty; just and true are thy ways, thou King of saints.

Revelation 15:1-3

What number is the enemy using? What number of demons are you up against? What is going to come against you first? And what will be second? After the first wave of attacks, what should you prepare for?

It is important to overcome the number of the beast. The number of the beast speaks of the formation or pattern the enemy will attack you with. Perhaps the best picture of this is found in soccer matches where the players have different patterns of play. The players do not just surge forward like a flock of eleven birds. The coach may send his players racing forward in a pattern of four, then another four, then two! Or he may send them in a pattern of four players, then five players; then, one last one. In other words you can expect a certain number of attackers to descend on you in a certain order.

Satan and the demons that hate us also come in patterns and numbers.

All through the Bible you see this pattern of demons operating in numbers and patterns to attack and invade humans. If you get some of these patterns right, you will understand what is happening to you when you are under attack.

Hardly is there anything like a solitary attack on you. It is important to know the team, the numbering and the type of demons that are being sent against you. Anyone who knows about lions knows that they do not work alone. Lions have well-coordinated group attacks. For instance, if you see one lion closing in on the left side, you should be concerned that other lions are probably nearby and coming in from another angle.

Demon Patterns

1. **The attack of the devil is likened to the attack of a lion.** Lions never attack alone. They move in packs with well-coordinated moves which reveal great intelligence.

Be sober, be vigilant; because your adversary the devil, as a roaring lion, walketh about, seeking whom he may devour:

1 Peter 5:8

2. **There were three devils that came out of the mouth of the beast and the false prophet.** This time, the devils came in a group of three.

And I saw three unclean spirits like frogs come out of the mouth of the dragon, and out of the mouth of the beast, and out of the mouth of the false prophet.

Revelation 16:13

3. **Jesus spoke of seven demons that are brought in to occupy a man after one demon is cast out of him.**

When the unclean spirit is gone out of a man, he walketh through dry places, seeking rest, and findeth none. Then he saith, I will return into my house from whence I came out; and when he is come, he findeth it empty, swept, and garnished.

Then goeth he, and taketh with himself seven other spirits more wicked than himself, and they enter in and dwell there: and the last state of that man is worse than the first. Even so shall it be also unto this wicked generation.

Matthew 12:43-45

4. **The mad man of Gadara had been invaded by a large pack of demons in their thousands.** This large pack of demons is called a legion of demons. A legion, in the days of Jesus, consisted of six thousand, eight hundred and twenty-six men. There were about six thousand demons in this man.

But when he saw Jesus afar off, he ran and worshipped him, and cried with a loud voice, and said, What have I to do with thee, Jesus, thou Son of the most high God? I adjure thee by God, that thou torment me not. For he said unto him, Come out of the man, thou unclean spirit. And he asked him, What is thy name? And he answered, saying, My name is Legion: for we are many.

Mark 5:6-9

5.   **The stealing, killing and destroying team has three demons that will work together against you.** There will hardly be an attack that has no follow up attacks. Lying demons, stealing demons and killing demons often move together, likewise you will hear of lying, stealing and killing always happening together. Jesus told us that the thief comes to steal, to kill and to destroy!

The thief cometh not, but for to steal, and to kill, and to destroy: I am come that they might have life, and that they might have it more abundantly.

John 10:10

The Secret of
the Five Realities

And I saw a new heaven and a new earth: for the first heaven and the first earth were passed away; and there was no more sea. And I John saw the holy city, new Jerusalem, coming down from God out of heaven, prepared as a bride adorned for her husband. And I heard a great voice out of heaven saying, Behold, the tabernacle of God is with men, and he will dwell with them, and they shall be his people, and God himself shall be with them, and be their God.

And God shall wipe away all tears from their eyes; and THERE SHALL BE NO MORE DEATH, NEITHER SORROW, NOR CRYING, NEITHER SHALL THERE BE ANY MORE PAIN: for the former things are passed away.

Revelation 21:1-4

And THERE SHALL BE NO MORE CURSE: but the throne of God and of the Lamb shall be in it; and his servants shall serve him:

Revelation 22:3

Τhe five realities of earthly life today are described in the verses above. They are death, sorrow, crying, pain and curses.

Implications of the Five Realities

1. *Death, sorrow, crying, pain and curses* exist on the earth today and characterize life on this earth. No matter what doctrine you hold, you will see that life has these characteristics. Anyone who is a man of faith will also see these realities. Who can honestly say he has lived on this earth and not seen the futility, the hunger, the pain and the sufferings of the masses?

2. If God has spared you some of the *death, sorrow, crying, pain and curses,* it is your duty to show comfort to the many who are experiencing these five realities in a real way. Our duty as Christians is to show compassion, love and care to all kinds of sorrows, pains, crying, death and curses that ravage the human race. God has called us to be comforters and helpers of those who are in prison, those who are sick, those who are naked, those who are hungry, those who are homeless and those who are thirsty. This is God's love in action to a race of rebellious and disobedient people.

3. The presence of *death, sorrow, crying, pain and curses* is the reason for the futility and hopelessness in the world in spite of advances, improvements and fantastic technology of our day. The presence of major worldwide curses is the reason for the anxiety, fear, confusion and chaos in this world.

4. If you understand *death, sorrow, crying, pain and curses,* you will not try too hard to create a world down here absent of these pains and sorrows. God has promised us wonderful mansions and rewards for eternity. Heaven is where our hope must be. The scriptures show us that there is coming a time when God will take these five things away from

the earth and from our lives. Painkillers are an important revelation of wisdom from God. God has provided the spirit of wisdom and knowledge as a standard of wisdom against the pains of this world.

5. If you truly understand *death, sorrow, crying, pain and curses* you will prepare for death on a daily basis. Death will not be a distant concern. Death will not be something that you leave for seventy year olds to think about. You, as a young man, will have it at the forefront of your mind and heart. You will prepare for it because you have the wisdom of God for it. People who have the wisdom of God about death are those who have serious discussions about death and what to do in the event of death. People who have the wisdom of God will have written wills, oral wills and spoken declarations about what to do whenever death strikes.

I know people who believe so much in the Word of God that they declare themselves to be immortal here and now. Such beliefs are mistakes that cause confusion in the minds of young Christians. We are not immortal now. We are frail, weak and in need of a lot of help. We are definitely not immortal.

There is no need to reject the reality of *death, sorrow, crying, pain and curses* on earth. That only makes these realities worse than they need be.

I know people who rejected the need to make wills because they rejected the idea that God would allow them to die. That will make your death more intolerable than it need be. Without accepting these realities, you will leave your family and church in great difficulty.

The Secret of the Name, the Number and the Image

And I saw another sign in heaven, great and marvellous, seven angels having the seven last plagues; for in them is filled up the wrath of God. I saw as it were a sea of glass mingled with fire: and them that had gotten the victory over the beast, and over his IMAGE, and over his mark, and over the NUMBER of his NAME, stand on the sea of glass, having the harps of God.

Revelation 15:1-2

The three noteworthy aspects of a leader are the name of the leader, the number of a leader and the image of a leader. These three advance him more than anything else.

Anyone who fights with you will present his name, a number, and an image!

Whoever you fight with will be coming at you with a name, a number and an image.

The name: A fight with the devil can be understood by the name with which the enemy fights. He may fight you as the "adversary" or as the "accuser " or as the "liar" or as the "murderer"! Whichever name is presented should tell you what to expect from the enemy.

The number: Also, the devil may come to you in a team of *three* devils ("And I saw three unclean spirits like frogs come out of the mouth of the dragon, and out of the mouth of the beast, and out of the mouth of the false prophet" Revelation 16:13), or a team of seven devils ("Then goeth he, and taketh with himself *seven* other spirits more wicked than himself, and they enter in and dwell there: and the last state of that man is worse than the first. Even so shall it be also unto this wicked generation" Matthew 12:45) or even a legion of devils ("And he asked him, what is thy name? And he answered, saying, my name is *Legion:* for we are many" Mark 5:9)!

The image: You must watch out for the image of the enemy. The pictures we see on television are part of satan's war on the people of God. Pornography is one of the vilest visual onslaughts on the Christian kingdom. Satan fights against the church with images.

Your Name, Your Number and Your Image

In your war against your enemy, it is important to develop a strong name, a strong image and a strong number.

You must have a good name with which to wage war. Some people do not have a good name for their churches and ministries. The name you use fights for you or may even fight against you.

Sometimes the name you have chosen is not clear enough and does not help your vision. When I began evangelistic crusades, I felt led to give a clear name that would generate faith for healing. Healing was to be a main aspect of the evangelistic ministry. So I used the name "*Healing Jesus Crusade*". I could have called it "*Dag's Evangelistic Crusade*". I could have called it "*Dag's Salvation Campaign*". I could have also called it "*The Gospel Razzmatazz*". These names would not have fought for me as well as the name "Healing Jesus Crusade". The name of Jesus and the word "Healing" together, form a powerful name.

You will notice the scripture speaks of those who were able to OVERCOME THE NAME AND THE NUMBER of the beast. When presented in areas that are hostile to Christianity the healing name is always victorious. People need healing. Even those who are antagonistic to Christ need healing. You need to wage war with a good name. Give a good name to your church. Give a good name to your gospel outreach. Give a good name to your child. Even give a good name to your dog. I know someone who called his guard-dog "Effective". That is a good name! The dog will be an effective guard.

It is also important to make war with a good image. Most people who do well in ministry have good photographs of themselves and are also engaged in good television work. The presentation of a good image wages a great war against the enemy. Pastors with huge billboards are fighting the war with their image. Many people are attracted and many come without knowing why. They do not know that an image has drawn them to the church.

You must fight with a good number! Many people are fighting with a single number "one". A pastor with a large ministry who does not have many good assistants is all alone. He is fighting with the number "one".

Many ministers do not have assistants and real helpers. A person who goes to war with a number of fighters is a greater fighter than someone who stands alone. An enemy who has many helpers is more dangerous than an enemy who stands alone.

For many ministries, satan just has to knock off one person and the ministry will be closed down. There are men of God who are actually like an octopus with many arms, legs and parts. Knocking out one little corner will not achieve much. Cutting off one of the eight long tentacles will not end the life of an octopus.

Satan is more afraid of a man of God who is actually a composite of many different people. That person represents other capable men who work with him. Think about it! A soccer team that comes to the World Cup Tournament with only one very good player is a different kind of team from those that come with eleven very good players.

Some teams have only one good player and even though he may be very good, the team is usually not able to accomplish much. Many countries have one very good player but it takes a team of eleven to do the job. Fighting with one is different from fighting with eleven.

What numbers are you fighting with? Are you alone? Are you the one and only jack-of-all-trades? Will your absence, death or departure spell the end of all things?

In my experience, fighting with a number of helpers and fighters, (some visible and some invisible) give far greater victories. It is time to rise up and raise mighty associates and helpers. It is time to fight in a team of eleven. It is time to stop fighting as a soloist.

The Secret of Dealing with a Devil

And I saw an angel come down from heaven, having the key of the bottomless pit and a great chain in his hand.

AND HE LAID HOLD ON THE DRAGON, THAT OLD SERPENT, WHICH IS THE DEVIL, AND SATAN, AND BOUND HIM a thousand years, AND CAST HIM INTO THE BOTTOMLESS PIT, AND SHUT HIM UP, AND SET A SEAL UPON HIM, that he should deceive the nations no more, till the thousand years should be fulfilled: and after that he must be loosed a little season.

Revelation 20:1-3

T

he way to deal with a devil is clearly unveiled in this great revelation. They bound him, shut him up and set a seal on him!

So where is the devil? How can we make contact with the devil so that we can bind him and shut him up?

Jesus answered them, Have not I chosen you twelve, and one of you is a devil?

He spake of Judas Iscariot the son of Simon: for he it was that should betray him, being one of the twelve.

John 6:70-71

This scripture teaches that a person who betrays you is a devil. What does it mean to have a devil in your church? To have a devil is to have a disloyal and unfaithful person in your life! That is what it means to have a devil in your church!

What God did to the devil is what you must do to all the "Judases" in your life and ministry. The book of Revelation teaches us four principles for dealing with disloyal and treacherous people.

Do not try to be wiser than God. Be followers of God. Do not be wise in your own conceits.

Be not wise in thine own eyes: fear the Lord, and depart from evil (Proverbs 3:7).

I remember a pastor who had a disloyal assistant. He travelled with his family for a few weeks, leaving the church of several thousand members with his associate. When he got back he found his church unstable with his associate deciding to resign. Unknown to him, this associate had spread many bad stories about him and made the church dislike its own head pastor. The associate insisted on resigning and to the utter amazement of the senior pastor, he left with almost the whole church. This pastor was left with about twenty members (including his own family). Such is the work of a disloyal assistant. An entire church was reduced from three thousand to twenty members.

If you make mistakes with the handling of a "Judas", you will only live to regret it. Devils, disloyal people and snakes are dangerous things. You must handle them with knowledge and with God's wisdom! You must only handle them God's way.

God used four mighty principles to deal with the devil. Binding them up, putting them in a bottomless pit, shutting them up and putting seals on them. Let's look at these four principles in a little detail.

1. **Bind up the devil in your church!** Binding a "Judas" is to restrict him. Some people actually allow such people to be free and to operate normally even after they know that they are disloyal. This is one of the great mistakes of those who are in leadership. Such leaders think they are walking in love and do not want to restrict anyone. If you do that, you are making yourself wiser than God.

2. **Put the devil in a bottomless pit!** This means that you must remove the foundation from under the feet of the rebellious person. The platform you have given them must be removed! Satan was put into a pit that had no bottom. No platform! No base!

   Remove the opportunity you have given the rebellious person to preach. Do not allow him to have the privileges and platforms he once had in your life and ministry. I remember one pastor who had a platform in the church. He spoke on radio, he spoke at conventions and spoke in our churches. But when he became a treacherous source of evil stories I took away that platform and he had no such platform to speak from anymore.

   No more preaching in our churches! No more invitations to our conventions! No more speaking on the radio!

   That is what a bottomless pit is! No more platforms to air your views!

3. **Shut the devil up!** Do not allow the voice of a rebellious person to be heard. Do not give such people any privileges of speaking to the people. Do not grant them access. Do not repeat their words! Do not repeat their sayings!

Such rebellious people are filled with stories and rumours to discredit you. Their aim is to belittle you and to blacken your reputation. Learn to silence the voice of the accuser by shutting him up out of sight.

Allowing accusers to speak is a very bad thing. Do not let them have the use of the microphone even once. Do not have a meeting to listen to their nonsense. Did God have a meeting with Lucifer to hear out his grievances? Not at all! Do not give accusers any such respect.

Do not give rebels the respect they want. Do not allow them to even state their case. It is useless to defend yourself against wicked accusations. It will get you nowhere! Your explanations and defences will not make them change their mind. I once allowed a rebellious person who was leaving the church to say goodbye to the congregation. He spoke with authority and declared his righteousness to the congregation. It was a great mistake. From then on, I do not allow rebellious people to speak to the church.

4. **Put a seal on the devil!** Make people aware of the dangers of a disloyal person. Tell them who exactly is the disloyal person and why he is disloyal. Let many people be aware of the dangers of such disloyal people. This is what it means to put a seal on the devil. Apostle Paul said; mark them and avoid them!

Now I beseech you, brethren, mark them which cause divisions and offences contrary to the doctrine which ye have learned; and avoid them (Romans 16:17).

How do you mark people? Have a meeting and tell those who matter the things that are happening so that they are not deceived by a disloyal operative. Tell them to avoid these people. Warn them of the dangers of associating with these disloyal people. Be specific. Mention the names of those involved so the people will know whom exactly is being disloyal, and what they are saying. If you leave people unmarked, they slip into the congregation and cause havoc. If God put a seal on the devil, why do you not want to put a seal on the rebels in your life? Are you wiser than God?

VICTORY SECRET NO. 34

The Secret of All Wars

And I saw **THREE UNCLEAN SPIRITS LIKE FROGS** come out of the mouth of the dragon, and out of the mouth of the beast, and out of the mouth of the false prophet.

For they are **THE SPIRITS OF DEVILS**, working miracles, which go forth unto the kings of the earth and of the whole world, **TO GATHER THEM TO THE BATTLE** of that great day of God Almighty.

Revelation 16:13-14

The ultimate trick of Satan is to make Christians fight against each other. The presence of devils is seen in the presence of conflicts and wars! Notice how three unclean spirits have only one aim: *to gather the nations to battle.*

When you understand that demons are the instigators of all conflicts, wars and battles, you will be unwilling to get involved in unnecessary wars. All marital conflicts, all wars, all church splits and conflicts are demon inspired.

Notice again, when the dragon was released from prison after a thousand years, he immediately organized a world war.

And when the thousand years are expired, Satan shall be loosed out of his prison,

And shall go out to deceive the nations which are in the four quarters of the earth, Gog and Magog, TO GATHER THEM TOGETHER TO BATTLE: the number of whom is as the sand of the sea.

And they went up on the breadth of the earth, and compassed the camp of the saints about, and the beloved city: and fire came down from God out of heaven, and devoured them.

Revelation 20:7-9

This is the main work of the devil: to get human beings to fight and destroy each other! To get couples to fight and destroy each other! To get churches to fight and destroy each other! To get pastors to fight and destroy each other. Be very careful when you see yourself being drawn into fights, conflicts and wars!

Satan's master plan is to get all nations to be at war. Satan is good at getting people to go to war. He can even get angels to fight with God the Creator!

Satan is able to get humans to even be at war with God. Why is Satan so good at making humans quarrel and be at war? The Bible reveals Satan's secret ability to create such conflicts and wars. He uses deception to get us to fight one another. What are the deceptions that are used to get us into war?

There are four main deceptions that work to bring about all wars.

1. **The deception about your own strengths and weaknesses.**
   When you are deceived about how strong you are, you are encouraged to enter into wars and conflicts. You are deceived that you will win. This is why nations organise military marches and display mighty weapons; to dissuade the enemy from thinking of attacking them. "See how powerful I am! Don't try attacking me" is what they seem to be saying!

2. **The deception about your enemy's strengths and weaknesses.** Often you are deceived about how weak your enemy is. Many people think they can quickly deal with the enemy. Soon they find out that the enemy is not as weak as they thought. Many spouses are deceived about the other spouse's determination not to be run over and pushed around in marriage. They start a conflict only to find out that they are in a titanic struggle of life and death.

3. **The deception about your moral rights to fight for something.** In churches, many feel they have a right to correct the pastor and correct the way the church is run. Some people feel they have moral right to control the lives and activities of their spouses. It is this feeling of moral justification that leads people into conflict and wars. This is the deception that satan capitalizes on to get us to fight one another. You feel justified about the war you are embarking on.

4. **The deception about the need to achieve something through a war.** Many also enter into wars and conflicts trying to build something, get something or achieve something. Hitler was trying to get more living space as he called it. Many Christians think they are achieving something as they correct men of God. However, you

cannot take the place of a judge. You cannot step into the judge's shoes and do his work. Watch out! You may be biting more than you can chew!

Without these four deceptions, Satan would not be able to get us to fight one another.

Have you been affected by any of these four deceptions? Are any of these four deceptions leading you to battle? Are you in a major conflict because you are deceived? Do you feel justified? Do you feel you are strong enough to win the arguments? Do you think the other party will not react? It is time to back down. Do not allow demons to gather you anymore into any battles!

Many of those who fight pastors and churches are deceived into going into war with even their own fathers. It is important to teach the Word of God in order to fight deceptions that lead people into unnecessary conflicts!

The Secret of
the Ten Kings

And there came one of the seven angels which had the seven vials, and talked with me, saying unto me, Come hither; I will shew unto thee the judgment of the great whore that sitteth upon many waters: With whom the kings of the earth have committed fornication, and the inhabitants of the earth have been made drunk with the wine of her fornication.

So he carried me away in the spirit into the wilderness: and I SAW A WOMAN SIT UPON A SCARLET COLOURED BEAST, FULL OF NAMES OF BLASPHEMY, HAVING SEVEN HEADS AND TEN HORNS.

Revelation 17:1-3

AND THE TEN HORNS WHICH THOU SAWEST ARE TEN KINGS, which have received no kingdom as yet; but receive power as kings one hour with the beast. THESE HAVE ONE MIND, AND SHALL GIVE THEIR POWER AND STRENGTH UNTO THE BEAST.

Revelation 17:12-13

The secret of the ten kings who made war with the Lamb is the secret of maximum unity. Most people experience fractional unity and maximum dispersal. They cannot unite to achieve anything no matter how important it is.

Maximum unity is the secret to the maximum impact of your vision. Because of satan's knowledge of maximum unity, he uses it in his fight against God and God's people. Satan seeks to divide us and disperse us all the time. He knows that we cannot achieve much on our own. Indeed the Bible says in Hebrews 11:40, "That they without us should not be made perfect". The perfection of our ministries will be complete when we are able to work together with *many* others for *many* years.

The secret of maximum unity can be used for good or evil. Satan's team used this key as revealed by the book of Revelation.

Indeed, the enemy knows so well that unity is vital that he constantly attacks our unity. Those who leave you, those who forget, those who pretend, those who are disloyal and those who are treacherous are just some of the agents who destroy unity in churches.

It is important to study the strategy of unity revealed in the beasts and evil creatures of the book of Revelation because it reveals some details on how unity works for maximum impact.

There are several points of unity between the ten kings spoken of in the revelation that achieved a high impact for evil. These points can be used by those of us who need to make a good impact and achieve great things for God.

These have ONE MIND, and shall give their power and strength unto the beast.

Revelations 17:13

For God hath put in their hearts to fulfil his will, and to agree, and give their kingdom unto the beast, until the words of God shall be fulfilled.

Revelations 17:17

The agreement of the ten kings and their decision to unite their power made them a noteworthy force that fought against the Lamb. These are the points of unity used by the kings to fight against the Lamb.

1. The ten kings have *one mind.*

2. The ten kings give their *power to one person.*

3. The ten kings give their *strength to one person.*

4. The ten kings *have it in their hearts to fulfill the will of God.*

5. The ten kings *have it in their hearts to agree!*

6. The ten kings have it in their hearts *to give their kingdom to one person.*

7. The ten kings take the steps of unity *until the words of God are fulfilled.*

The key of unity is revealed by studying the strategy of the ten kings. This strategy of unity hinges on giving power to one person. This strategy of unity hinges on agreeing instead of debating and arguing.

I have experienced and exercised the power of unity in my ministry for many years. Many of my pastors agree with me and trustingly give their power to me to build the church. I could not have gone very far on my own. The loving trust and confidence of many pastors in my leadership has enabled me to come thus far!

I once advised a group of churches that were independent of each other, to come together, to agree, and to give their power to one person. In so doing, they would be able to accomplish much more for the Lord. They could pull their resources together and concentrate on building one cathedral at a time. After one was complete, they would then join forces and build another one.

Unfortunately, many things keep us in our own corners.

Indeed, pride keeps us apart!

Fear keeps us from obeying the command to unite and work together!

Backbiting keeps us apart!

Lack of strength in leaders keeps us apart! Leaders who fail to see the need to unite do not make the great efforts needed to make unity work.

Wives making negative comments and suggestions to their husbands at home keep ministers apart!

Whisperers keep people apart!!

When will we realize the need to set aside differences and begin to agree? Many of us will arrive in Heaven to find out that much more was expected of us than we actually did.

The Secret of Revelation and Angels

THE REVELATION of Jesus Christ, which God gave unto him, to shew unto his servants things which must shortly come to pass; and HE SENT AND SIGNIFIED IT BY HIS ANGEL UNTO HIS SERVANT JOHN: who bare record of the word of God, and of the testimony of Jesus Christ, and of all things that he saw.

Revelation 1:1-2

The book of Revelation was given to John through angelic activity. The whole of the book of Revelation was shown to John by an angel. Wherever there is revelation there are angels. How exactly do angels bring revelation? How exactly does a revelation come? I don't know! There is no need to try to understand how these angels work. But I believe the Word of God. The spirit of revelation is greatly associated with angels. You will notice in the scripture that the revelation that was sent to John was sent by an angel.

Once, as I was holding a pastors' conference, there was a lady in the meeting whose eyes were opened. She saw a host of angels in the conference room whilst I was ministering. She was so moved by this vision. Although I have not seen angels myself, a lot of people have seen angelic activity around me. Watch out for people who are endued with revelation. They usually have heavy angelic activity in their lives!

Kenneth Hagin received a lot of revelation from God. He shared many times about how angels appeared to him and brought help from God. Great men of God usually have many angels operating around them.

1.   The seven churches received their messages through angels.

There is angelic activity where there is revelation. Remember that great revelation is usually associated with the presence of angels. Anyone who has a lot of revelation has a lot of angels around him.

Unto the angel of the church of Ephesus write; These things saith he that holdeth the seven stars in his right hand, who walketh in the midst of the seven golden candlesticks;

Revelation 2:1

And unto the angel of the church in Smyrna write; These things saith the first and the last, which was dead, and is alive;

Revelation 2:8

And to the angel of the church in Pergamos write; These things saith he which hath the sharp sword with two edges;

Revelation 2:12

And unto the angel of the church in Thyatira write; These things saith the Son of God, who hath his eyes like unto a flame of fire, and his feet are like fine brass;

Revelation 2:18

And unto the angel of the church in Sardis write; These things saith he that hath the seven Spirits of God, and the seven stars; I know thy works, that thou hast a name that thou livest, and art dead.

Revelation 3:1

And to the angel of the church in Philadelphia write; These things saith he that is holy, he that is true, he that hath the key of David, he that openeth, and no man shutteth; and shutteth, and no man openeth;

Revelation 3:7

And unto the angel of the church of the Laodiceans write; These things saith the Amen, the faithful and true witness, the beginning of the creation of God;

Revelation 3:14

2.   The little book was delivered through angels.

The whole of the tenth chapter of Revelation is about a little book that was given to John. This little book was brought to John by the largest angel ever seen or heard of. John's ministry was about to be transformed. He was about to be launched out to speak to many people, many nations, many tongues, and even kings. John's great ministry was taken to the highest level by the gift of a book that he received. This book came to his hand through an angel. Angels may be involved when God is leading you to important books. When God wants to bless you, He will often send you a book. Books are very important for your ministry. Watch how John received this little book from this mighty angel.

> **And I saw another mighty angel come down from heaven, clothed with a cloud: and a rainbow was upon his head, and his face was as it were the sun, and his feet as pillars of fire: And he had in his hand a little book open: and he set his right foot upon the sea, and his left foot on the earth,**
>
> **Revelation 10:1-2**

> **And the voice which I heard from heaven spake unto me again, and said, Go and take the little book which is open in the hand of the angel which standeth upon the sea and upon the earth.**
>
> **And I went unto the angel, and said unto him, Give me the little book. And he said unto me, Take it, and eat it up; and it shall make thy belly bitter, but it shall be in thy mouth sweet as honey.**
>
> **And I took the little book out of the angel's hand, and ate it up; and it was in my mouth sweet as honey: and as soon as I had eaten it, my belly was bitter. And he said unto me, Thou must prophesy again before MANY PEOPLES, AND NATIONS, AND TONGUES, AND KINGS.**
>
> **Revelation 10:8-11**

VICTORY SECRET NO.37

The Secret of Reading, Hearing and Keeping

The Revelation of Jesus Christ, which God gave unto him, to shew unto his servants things which must shortly come to pass; and he sent and signified it by his angel unto his servant John: Who bare record of the word of God, and of the testimony of Jesus Christ, and of all things that he saw.

BLESSED IS HE THAT READETH, AND THEY THAT HEAR THE WORDS OF THIS PROPHECY, AND KEEP THOSE THINGS WHICH ARE WRITTEN therein: for the time is at hand.

Revelation 1:1-3

A great blessing comes to anyone who is given a revelation. You must pray that God will bless you with "revelation". To receive the blessing of a revelation, there are some things you must do. God will change your life when you receive His wisdom.

1. The blessing of a revelation comes to you by hearing.

A wise man will HEAR, and will increase learning; ...

Proverbs 1:5

A revelation is the greatest blessing you could ever have. Every revelation carries a mighty blessing with it. The great revelation that transformed my life, came to me by *HEARING*. In 1988, I was a medical student in my final year. One night, whilst praying, I had a great revelation. The revelation was simple: "From today, you can teach." I heard a voice in the room say, "From today, you can teach." God revealed to me that He had given me the gift of teaching. He also revealed to me that the gift would be in operation from that day. That revelation changed my whole life!

BLESSED IS HE that readeth, and they THAT HEAR the words of this prophecy, and keep those things which are written therein: for the time is at hand.

Revelation 1:3

Instead of being excited that I was finishing Medical School in a few months, I was now excited that I was anointed to teach the Word of God. When God gave me the revelation that I could teach His word, it came along with a worldwide ministry, a salary, a house, cars, employees and everything I would ever have. That is the power of a revelation! Don't ever trivialise or minimise the power of receiving a revelation through hearing.

2. **The blessing of revelation comes to you by reading.**

BLESSED IS HE THAT READETH, and they that hear the words of this prophecy, and keep those things which are written therein: for the time is at hand.

Revelation 1:3

The blessing of a revelation also comes through *READING*. A different kind of blessing comes through reading. Reading gives a deeper and clearer understanding of a revelation. Hearing leads to quicker understanding for your soul. For the details of a revelation and the mature appreciation of a revelation you need to move from hearing into reading.

3. **The blessing of revelation comes to you by keeping it.**

BLESSED IS HE THAT readeth, and they that hear the words of this prophecy, and KEEP THOSE THINGS which are written therein: for the time is at hand.

Revelation 1:3

The blessing of a revelation also comes by *KEEPING* it. Keeping the revelation involves protecting it from disappearing. The word "keep" speaks of protection. It means "to guard something properly by keeping the eye on it" and "providing a fortress with full military protection". Revelation is so important that it deserves full-militarized protection. Because entire ministries are birthed through revelation, revelation is seen as a very dangerous thing to the devil and he fights revelation constantly. As time goes by, people tend to water down revelation that has been received. It is important to protect the ideas and the revelations that God has given to His church. How can we do this?

The first way to keep a revelation is to hear it again and again.

Repeatedly hearing and repeatedly reading, protects the revelation from going away. I have preached and taught many sermons and revelations. It is only the ones that I have taught repeatedly that have stayed with my hearers. I have read many wonderful books that contained many wonderful revelations. However, it is only the books that I have read repeatedly that have stayed with me and benefited me in a certain way.

I laugh at people who listen to sermons only once. I smile at people who read books only once. The scripture teaches us to hear, to read and to *keep the revelation* that is given to us.

You may hear a revelation, you may read a revelation but if you do not keep it by repetitively hearing it or reading it, it will slip away from you. The books that have benefited me are the books I have read continuously for ten years and more. The great teachings of Kenneth Hagin, which have benefitted me immensely, are the ones that I have listened to repetitively over a period of many years.

The second way to keep a revelation is by writing it down.

WRITE the things which thou hast seen, and the things which are, and the things which shall be hereafter;

Revelation 1:19

Books are important because, they are the preservation of revelation. I have preached many great sermons and taught many wonderful things. But it is only the revelations I have written down that have stayed in the church and have been protected from disappearing.

Sometimes, I preach an amazing sermon and I think to myself, "This is the greatest revelation I have ever taught." But a few weeks later, I am unable to remember what I taught. Books are the greatest preservers of revelation for the church. The Bible is a marvellous book containing revelation that was written down and preserved for us for 6000 years. We would not know anything about King David, Abraham, Isaac or Jacob if it were not for the Bible. We would not have any idea of how the earth was created if it were not for the Bible.

Unguarded revelation leaks away and is found no more! When you have a dream and you do not write it down, it disappears in no time. Whilst you are having the dream, it seems so real, so amazing and so vivid. But if you do not write it down it slips away.

I once attended the funeral of an important person. I went around his coffin and paid my last respects. The corpse had on a grey suit and was facing upwards with its eyes closed. I shook hands with everybody who mattered and left the funeral grounds. It was several weeks later, when I was reading through some dreams and visions I had written down that I realized that I had seen this man's funeral in a dream. It was a vivid dream that had woken me up at 3.00 am. However, it had completely slipped away from my memory and I only remembered it when I read through the visions and dreams God had given to me. If you want to guard your revelation, you must write it down!

The third way to keep a revelation is by obeying what has been revealed to you. Make sure you follow and obey the revelation God gives you. When I received the revelation that I could teach the Word of God, I began to teach and preach. I have tried to obey the revelation and walk in it. Through teaching and preaching, many churches have been established and the revelation is spreading.

The Secret of Writing Christian Books

I was in the Spirit on the Lord's day, and heard behind me a great voice, as of a trumpet,

Saying, I am Alpha and Omega, the first and the last: and, WHAT THOU SEEST, WRITE IN A BOOK, AND SEND IT UNTO THE SEVEN CHURCHES which are in Asia; unto Ephesus, and unto Smyrna, and unto Pergamos, and unto Thyatira, and unto Sardis, and unto Philadelphia, and unto Laodicea.

Revelation 1:10-11

The secret of writing Christian books is revealed in the book of Revelation. The commission to write books is seen in the book of Revelation. The book of Revelation clearly reveals and unveils things that are hidden from open view. Things that are not obvious are made known to us if we care to accept them. *Revelation means to unveil and to show something that is hidden.* These scriptures reveal why and how Christian books must be written.

Write a book because you have been instructed by the Lord to write. John did not make the mistake of writing when God had not asked him to write. One of satan's strategies to keep people away from important revelation is to make a lot of useless publications available to Christians.

This is the principle that the zebra uses to stay alive. One of the reasons why lions are not able to catch zebras is because of their numerous black stripes. These moving black stripes form a confusing image to the lion and they are unable to catch any particular zebra. In the end, the lion moves away from the herd of zebras in confusion and takes on something simpler without so many patterns. It simply cannot pick out the right zebra to kill. Similarly, the plethora of Christian literature makes it difficult for anyone to pick the right book.

Do not write books because everybody is writing. You are supposed to do things God tells you to do and not things that everyone else is doing. Do not consider writing a book as a mark of your spiritual rank. Neither John the Baptist nor Jesus Christ wrote books. Jesus told us that John the Baptist was the greatest prophet that ever lived. Jesus Christ was the Son of God Himself. Yet He never wrote a book. Are you trying to tell me that Paul was greater than Jesus because he wrote a book? Do not think that writing a book makes you a great man of God. That is a mistake. Write books because God tells you to write them.

You must write books to the church and for the church! Many pastors are deluded into thinking that they are messengers to the world. They are so excited when they have secular leaders and bank managers reading their books. The New Testament ministry of writing began two thousand years ago. The apostle John was specifically asked to write the book of Revelation and make it available to existing churches. Writing books (long letters) is nothing new. God has called some people to write certain books and send them to the churches.

Some years ago, the Lord asked me to write books. I was hesitant about it because I felt no one would read a book I had written. He asked me to employ someone to work on books if I was serious about obeying Him. This, I did, and today I have millions of books in print.

Saying, I am Alpha and Omega, the first and the last: and, What thou seest, WRITE IN A BOOK, AND SEND IT UNTO THE SEVEN CHURCHES which are in Asia; unto Ephesus, and unto Smyrna, and unto Pergamos, and unto Thyatira, and unto Sardis, and unto Philadelphia, and unto Laodicea.

Revelation 1:11

The long lasting letters are the letters that were written to the churches. Paul's letters to the churches are what we call the books of Corinthians, Philippians, Thessalonians, etc. Have the church in mind when you are writing. Do not have the secular world in mind when you are writing a book. Do not write books for secular purposes. Do not write books to businessmen for their financial benefit. If they want to glean from the wisdom of the Bible or the spiritual wisdom of your books let them come and read it for themselves. Then they will learn about business by learning about ministry.

It is a great mistake to write books without sending them to the churches. Send the books to the churches. Sending books to the churches is different from selling the books to the churches. Your writings will ensure that your members have the written word to support what they have heard.

Do not write theoretical books about things you have not experienced.

"What thou seest, write in a book..." John was told to write books about what he had seen. Your books will only be interesting when they are about things you have experienced. When an experienced person is talking, it is much more interesting to listen, to hear and to receive. Paul, the apostle, wrote to the churches and addressed real issues that he understood. He knew what he was talking about and his books are still the most powerful Christian books in circulation today.

It is sad to see many of us trying to write books about things we do not know. It is sad to see poor people writing books about how to prosper. It is sad to see defeated people writing about how to be victorious.

Write books as a ministry and not as a business. Do not allow the "mark" of buying and selling for profit to be on your ministry. John was not commissioned to write books by the god of this world. He was commissioned by Almighty God to write and to make his writings available to the churches. John did not make the mistake of turning the production of the book of Revelation into a business.

Can you imagine if John had made the writing of the book of Revelation a business? He would have kept the book of Revelation and released it only to those who could pay for it. Most of us would never have received nor heard of the book of Revelation. John would have destroyed his ministry if he had turned the book of Revelation into a business. "Freely you received, freely give" (Matthew 10:8 - NASB). The ministry of writing is just like the ministry of preaching and teaching. All the rules that apply to the ministry of preaching and teaching apply to the ministry of writing books.

To the making of many books there is no end!

References

1. Boundless. "Antibiotic Discovery." *Boundless Microbiology Boundless,* 26 May. 2016. Retrieved 25 Jan. 2017 from https://www.boundless.com/microbiology/textbooks/boundless-microbiology-textbook/antimicrobial-drugs-13/overview-of-antimicrobial-therapy-153/antibiotic-discovery-772-5017/

2. Booth, William. "A Vision Of The Lost By William Booth (1829-1912)". *Aibi.ph. N.p.*, 2017. Web. 25 Jan. 2017 retrieved from https://www.aibi.ph/downloads/Church%20History%20Documents/William%20Booth%20vision1.htm